JUSTICE,
LEGAL SYSTEMS, and
SOCIAL STRUCTURE

H. RICHARD HARTZLER

JUSTICE, LEGAL SYSTEMS, and SOCIAL STRUCTURE

KENNIKAT PRESS
Port Washington, N. Y. • London
A DUNELLEN PUBLISHING COMPANY BOOK

TO LIZ, SCOTT, TODD, AND SUSAN

Printed in the United States of America

Distributed in United States and Canada by
Kennikat Press, Port Washington, N. Y. 11050

Distributed in British Commonwealth (except Canada) by
Martin Robertson & Company Ltd., London

Library of Congress Cataloging in Publication Data

Hartzler, H   Richard, 1928–
    Justice, legal systems, and social structure.

    "A Dunellen Publishing Company book."
    Bibliography: p.
    Includes index.
    1. Sociological jurisprudence. 2. Justice,
Administration of. I. Title.
Law   340   76-7360
ISBN 0-8046-7079-X

CONTENTS

LIST OF CASES

LIST OF CHARTS

PREFACE

The message of this book is dependent on the work of the following scholars: Harold D. Lasswell, Neil J. Smelser, Roscoe Pound, Karl Llewelly Adamson Hoebel, Max Weber, Robert A. Dahl, and Charles E. Lindblom. It integrates and builds on their efforts. No mere reporting of the works of others is intended, however, The integrated theory of the nature of justice, legal systems, and social structures is the author's, who assumes full responsibility for it as developed herein.

The first chapter takes Lasswell's primary and instrumental goals constructs and develops them in a way that makes them relevant to law–government structure and processes. A goal that is neither primary nor instrument but is a principal concern in this work is added. That goal is justice. As the is a relationship between primary and instrumental goals, there is also a relationship between them and justice. A proposal of an approximation of justice is presented on a continuum.

In Chapter 2, the essence of the postulated approximation of justice is translated into the strain concept employed in relationship to role theory in sociology. The concepts of role theory, functional exigencies, strains and reactions to strain, social structure and control, attitudinal and behavior change—all founded on descriptions by Smelser, Dahl, and Lindblom—are used as a base to connect justice with social engineering and behavior. By the end of Chapter 2 the nature of justice and social structure and a simple relationship between the two has been developed.

The third basic element of this work, a legal system, is included in Chapter 3. Llewellyn is the principal source of the nature of legal systems. The idea is presented that legal systems exist in most groups and that all persons occupy one of four power positions in every group. It is on the basis of this position that are found the opportunities or limitations for individual effectiveness in social problem solving. Pound's concept of the social engineering process is personified in the social engineer. His power bases, roles, sense of justice and injustice (strain), and activities are integrated within the context of social structure, and finally it is demonstrated that his quest for justice is basic to group activity.

In Chapter 4, more of Llewellyn's ideas about legal systems are blended with Pound's jural postulates and theory of interests. These are then blended with Lasswell's primary and instrumental goals. Then the idea of justice is related to the product. The entire collection of concepts is integrated with social structure and social engineering behavior.

Though no chapter is based on the work of Dahl and Lindblom, to this point the reader will have been exposed to some of their ideas about goals, calculation and control for problem solving, and bargaining as a socioeconomic process. These ideas and others are carried on and integrated into the succeeding chapters as well.

Chapter 5 blends some of Llewellyn's ideas about law-government with some of Weber's most important theories of law finding and application, before Llewellyn's functions of law-government are employed in Chapter 6. Therein, those functions are related to Pound's jural postulates and social interest theories. The whole is then tied to instrumental and primary goals and to justice.

In Chapter 7 decision-making processes are analyzed. The impact of social structure on the decision maker is dealt with on the conscious level and, particularly, below the level of consciousness. Much is made of Holmes' idea that an inarticulate major premise plays a major role in decision making. The relationship of an inarticulate major premise in a legal system with social structure and justice provides the final representation of the theory of this book—that is, the relationship of justice, legal systems and social structure—or justice, law and order.

There are many diagrams, flow charts, and models within these chapters. They are not intended as mere pictures of the verbalizations of the chapters. They are intended to help one understand what has been written to some extent. But, because the writing is simple enough, the diagrams are intended more as elaborations, sources of more information and prods to thought and understanding. This book is a small one primarily because the diagrams have been relied upon to carry a considerable burden for conveying the message. (The author hopes to publish a book about business and its environment that depends almost entirely on such diagrams—when the time is right.) It is, of course, recognized that such drawings are abstract and artificial, but so are all generalizations about reality. Holmes once said that "no generalization is worth a damn, including this one." He overstated the case. All knowledge is in the form of generalizations. He was right to the extent that he recognized that generalizations are approximations of reality, with all the defects of omission and commission. The diagrams contained herein may in some cases overstate reality. Others may understate it. Attempts have been made to avoid the extremes of either. If the reader will make allowances for their deficiencies and appreciate their efficiencies, this work will say more to him. The diagrams are a form of knowledge generalization.

Chapter 8 is an exercise which permits the reader to test for himself whether this work has value for him.

The following people deserve my gratitude and recognition for the parts they played in the development of this book: the people of the Commonwealth of Massachusetts, whose taxes pay my salary in part to do this sort of thing; the Administrators and Trustees of the University of Massachusetts who made the decision to award a sabbatical providing me with enough time to complete the project; my colleagues who carried the burden of my classes during that time; and Vesta Powers, Susan Pearson, and Margaret Anderson, who typed the manuscript.

JUSTICE,
LEGAL SYSTEMS, and
SOCIAL STRUCTURE

INTRODUCTION

Challenge a person to speak more than ten words on the subject of justice. He probably will not meet the challenge. For most, the articulation of feelings is difficult, and it is feelings that are their basic justice experiences, not verbalized generalizations. When one senses the justice or injustice of a situation, he may quickly recognize it and label it as such; but such labeling is about the limit of common experience in articulating justice. One is seldom surprised to find others who share his sense of justice. They understand one another without communicating. What is surprising is to encounter someone who senses justice in a situation about which one has just sensed injustice. The two may argue about the merits of the situation, but they will probably not explore what each means by justice and injustice. If after the discussion they do not share a common view of the merits of the situation, each more than likely views the other as having something wrong with him, after which he is dismissed as unimportant or feared as dangerous.

The scholarly studies of justice rarely concern themselves with what justice really is. Edmund Cahn[1] and Jean Piaget[2] are exceptions. But many others simply use the word as descriptive of the existence or operation of a legal system. Gordon Tullock[3] hates to use the word itself and certainly would never explore its meaning. For him that would be a waste of time. A common impression from all this is that justice is a matter of law and legal procedure, that there is no justice without law or except as law has played a role.

Justice is not an invention of law or necessarily even descriptive of law, legal processes, or outcomes. It is an important human goal, but it means different things to different people. Rarely, as with most goals, is it achieved. Rarely, also, is there complete failure to achieve any part of the goal. Mysteriously, some sense justice when others sense injustice. More mysteriously, one may sense justice during the course of an event and sense injustice about the same event at a later time, as his memory causes him to reexperience it. The desire to sense justice in events may cause people to look to law as an instrument to control those events. Then justice has preceded law. Law is made a part of events and is itself then viewed as promoting or blocking justice, depending on the role it plays and also depending on the perceived self-interest of the participants in, or viewers of, the events.

In the events of their lives, those who perceive themselves as advantaged by the roles of a legal system usually assume that law produces justice and that the existence of justice is dependent on the existence of law. Those who perceive themselves as disadvantaged by a legal system may not, to the contrary, assume that law produces injustice. Taking notice of this further fact, the advantaged are reinforced in their beliefs that justice is a product of a legal system, any legal system, and any law. What is overlooked is that each may share essentially the same values and goals, which may more exactly explain their similar senses of justice than the explanation that law is a source of that justice.

Just what part shared values and goals as well as disparate values and goals play in common and differing senses of justice and injustice needs some consideration. Those who call for "law and order" are insensitive to the problem. Their approach to justice is simplistic—justice is a product of law and order. The term "law and order" is also simplistically understood by law and order advocates. For them, laws are the rules of the government to which the good citizen is obedient. Order is a peaceful condition due to an absence of crime. Law does justice to get order. Such a reasoner needs no ability to articulate the nature of justice. Social psychology, to them, is for the professors; and it certainly has nothing to do with the problem. Law is rules—there is no need to contemplate the complexities of a legal system, what it is, how it works, why it works or does not work, who operates it and why, to what ends and by what techniques. The fact that order is as complicated as social structure with all its variations and mysteries is not imagined. If a book is entitled *Justice, Legal Systems, and Social Structure,* the typical law and order advocate is not likely to recognize that it is about one of his favorite subjects.

This book explores the currently popular subject "law and order." It attempts to do so without the crippling simplicities just summarized, but instead in a realistic way. It purports to say more than ten words about justice. It purports to explore the nature, functions, and limitations of legal systems. It purports to introduce a relationship between justice, legal systems, and social structure in a way never done before. It purports to demonstrate to the reader that knowledge about justice is useful, that the quality of life of the reader and of men generally can be improved with it.

Three principal subjects—justice, social structure and legal systems—are integrated in this work. First the foundations and nature of justice are developed and are briefly related to social structure and law. Then social structure is examined and related to the subjects "justice" and "social engineering." After that, elements characteristic of all legal systems are explained and related more carefully to justice, social structure, and social engineering. By this point, it will have been made clear that justice is a concern of men associated together, that social structure almost inevitably requires a supporting legal system, and that legal systems can be found in all groups, state and nonstate.

The virtual inevitability of legal systems as a concept is then enlarged upon by means of an analysis of the relationship of conflict and goals. The idea of a legal system is further enlarged and identified as a law-government system so that one can better see the potential for such a system, because of its nature and complexity, either to contribute to one's sense of justice or injustice. The next part of this work demonstrates how this potential is realized one way or the other as the law-government system functions. It will become apparent that conflict generated by efforts at goal achievement makes law-government systems necessary and that such systems use conflict as opportunity building blocks to fashion parts of social structure for better goal achievement from the point of view of those in control. Throughout, the relationships of justice, legal systems, and social structure are of paramount importance.

The last part of the work focuses on the decision maker. It explains how he comes to use decision techniques more or less appropriate to goal achievement as conflict opportunities arise. It demonstrates the role that social structure and social psychology play in the process.

The goal of the book is to provide a hint about the relationships of fields of law, political science, sociology, anthropology, psychology, and the arts as a basis for more specific and detailed research by scholars in those fields. But it has been written for the citizen as well. With the knowledge contained herein, he may become a master of law as a tool for goal achievement, which is the other side of the coin from his role as a sometimes reluctant but obedient servant of the law. Certainly he will be able to speak more than ten words on the subject of "justice."

NOTES

1. Edmond N. Cahn, *The Sense of Injustice: An Anthropocentric View of Law* (New York: New York University Press, 1949).

2. Jean Piaget, *The Moral Judgment of the Child* (New York: Free Press, 1969).

3. Gordon Tullock, *The Logic of Law* (New York: Basic Books, 1971).

1

JUSTICE

Mark Twain knew something: Law and justice are not necessarily compatible. In a beautiful passage from *Huckleberry Finn* he revealed a paradox about law and justice. To act justly should make me feel good, and to act according to the law should also provide its satisfactions. But one may act according to his sense of justice and contrary to the law. How then does he feel?

Jim talked out loud all the time while I was talking to myself. He was saying how the first thing he would do when he got to a free state he would go to saving up money and never spend a single cent, and when he got enough he would buy his wife, which was owned on a farm close to where Miss Watson lived; and then they would both work to buy the two children, and if their master wouldn't sell them, they'd get an Ab'litionist to go and steal them.

It most froze me to hear such talk. He wouldn't ever dared to talk such talk in his life before. Just see what a difference it made in him the minute he judged he was about free. It was according to the old saying, "Give a nigger an inch and he'll take a ell." Thinks I, this is what comes of my not thinking. Here was this nigger, which I had as good as helped to run away, coming right out flat-footed and saying he would steal his children—children that belonged to a man I didn't even know, a man that hadn't ever done me no harm.

I was sorry to hear Jim say that, it was such a lowering of him. My conscience got to stirring me up hotter than ever, until at last I says to it, "Let up on me—it ain't too late yet—I'll paddle ashore at the first light and tell." I felt easy and happy and light as a feather right off. All my troubles was gone. I went to looking out sharp for a light, and sort of singing to myself. By and by one showed. Jim sings out:

"We's safe, Huck, we's safe! Jump up and crack yo' heels! Dat's de good ole Cairo at las', I jis knows it!"

I says:

"I'll take the canoe and go and see, Jim. It mightn't be, you know."

He jumped and got the canoe ready, and put his old coat in the bottom for me to set on, and give me the paddle; and as I shoved off, he says:

"Pooty soon I'll be a-shout'n' for joy, en I'll say, it's all on accounts of o'Huck; I's a free man, en I couldn't ever ben free ef it hadn't ben for Huck; Huck done it. Jim won't ever forgit you, Huck; you's de bes' fren' Jim's ever had; en you's de *only* fren old Jim's got now."

I was paddling off, all in a sweat to tell on him; but when he says this, it seemed to kind of take the tuck all out of me. I went along slow then, and I warn't right down certain whether I was glad I started or whether I warn't. When I was fifty yards off, Jim says:

"Dah you goes, de ole true Huck' de on'y white genlman dat kep' his promise to ole Jim."

Well, I just felt sick. But I says, I *got* to do it—I can't get *out* of it. Right then along comes a skiff with two men in it with guns, and they stopped and I stopped. One of them says:

"What's that yonder?"

"A piece of a raft," I says.

"Do you belong on it?"

"Yes, sir."

"Any men on it?"

"Only one, sir."

"Well, there's five niggers run off to-night up yonder, above the head of that bend. Is your man white or black?"

I didn't answer up prompt. I tried to, but the words wouln't come. I tried for a second or two to brace up and out with it, but I warn't man enough—hadn't the spunk of a rabbit. I see I was weakening; so I just give up trying, and up and says:

"He's white. . . ."

". . . If you see any runaway niggers you get help and nab them, and you can make some money by it."

"Good-by, sir," says I; "I won't let no runaway niggers get by me if I can help it."

They went off and I got aboard the raft, feeling bad and low, because I knowed very well I had done wrong, and I see it warn't no use for me to try to learn to do right; a body that don't get *started* right when he's little ain't got no show—when the pinch comes there ain't nothing to back him up and keep him to his work, and so he gets beat. Then I thought a minute, and says to myself, hold on; s'pose you'd 'a' done right and give Jim up, would you felt better than what you do now? No, says I, I'd feel just the same way I do now. Well, then, says I, what's the use you learning to do right when it's troublesome to do right and ain't no trouble to do wrong, and the wages is just the same?[1]

The passage speaks for itself.

It is obvious that a law deprived Jim of his freedom. As a free man he imagined working to earn money to buy his wife and children, all within the law. However, abetted by Huck, he was violating a law to achieve that freedom to act. Furthermore Jim's imagination was quickly taking him from the realm of freedom to the outer regions of license as he speculated about stealing his children. He was already anticipating that another law might block his ability to get what he wanted and that he would have to disregard that law if he could not make a contract to buy his children. Jim's desire is freedom for himself, his wife, and his children. To achieve that desire all of them must be in a place where the law will not permit them to be regarded as property for the use of others. If such law exists in some place, it promotes his desire to be free. It must exist or he cannot feel free.

His inclination to steal his children is viewed as ominous by Huck, the very person who is helping him escape slavery. Huck patently recognizes a commitment to the person who owns Jim's children and latently recognizes a commitment to the law, which supports that person's claim to the children. Huck's emotional reaction is interesting. Is he sensing injustice in his act of aiding Jim to escape slavery as he becomes uncomfortably aware of the chain of consequences he may have set loose? He attempts to create a rectitude which will make him feel much better as he paddles off to turn Jim in. He becomes happy and light as a feather as he contemplates doing right. He is about to make himself free—free of the burden of his criminal act. Surely, obedience to law is freedom—for Huck.

FREEDOM

"Obedience to Law is Freedom." The inscription on a sign posted over the entrance to a military stockade was for all to see. Apparently the person responsible for the sign felt that he had captured a fundamental truth essential to American life and was driven by dedication and good conscience to bring the message to all who passed by.

Some relationship exists between law and freedom: Law is necessary to the existence of freedom or law impinges on freedom or there is no relationship between law and freedom. Perhaps none of the expressions is totally true or untrue. To achieve precision and completeness of expression on the matter would be a vexing problem. But one conclusion is irresistible: In each statement the words "freedom" and "law" have different connotations for the utterer. The sense of freedom and of law is different for the adherent of each view.

One notion about freedom is that it is just an abstraction. For each person it differs on a subjective level. It differs for Jim, Huck, the men in the boat, and the person who owns Jim's children. Each person must contend with the problem of whose sense of freedom is to prevail when differing notions lead to conflict. There can be no correct notion in the extremely relativistic world he sees; so, correctness is out as a criterion for resolving the conflict. If there is a basis for compromise, compromise can be the tool of conflict resolution. It depends upon how highly individualistic and non-generalizable the senses of freedom of the parties to the conflict are. Or, conversely, it depends on the existence of similarities. The stronger is likely to prevail over the other. His sense of freedom will be gratified. The other will experience a deprivation of freedom.

The scale of conflict can be magnified as one group of those who perceive similarities in their senses of freedom finds its notions in conflict with those of another group. At the time of Huck's story, some northerners sensed a threat to their own freedom in the institution of slavery, while some southerners viewed slavery as necessary to avoid the labor and common problems of life from which they wanted to be free.[2] More compromise or greater strength exerted can be the technique for resolution of what could be an acute social conflict. Enforcement of compromise or the will of the stronger in complex society usually requires a specialized enforcer such as the police or the army.

Armies were resorted to by the North and the South to settle the slavery question. The North was going to impose its law on the South by assuring that it required all men to refrain from laying property claims against the lives of fellow human beings. In this respect, it is clear that law was viewed as necessary for the existence of freedom.

It is a noble purpose and effort of man to attempt to secure freedoms for himself and his fellow man by employing his law toward that end. Then another problem arises: Can those who believe the law is necessary to the existence of freedom maintain a social system facilitating freedom if they use specialized enforcers who believe that obedience to law is freedom? The military mind that elicited this proposition is an example of such an enforcer. Perhaps his is the better view for one with his specialty. Perhaps he could not do his job well if he shared the more expansive view of the larger society which he serves. The problem needs some basic empirical research. A dichotomy of prescribed and operational freedom could occur. Obviously social machinery adequate to appropriate staffing of a specialized enforcement function is necessary. Finally, is it obvious that a highly individualized and relativistic theory of the nature of freedom is least likely to afford a basis for coping with such problems?

Some no doubt feel that availability of choice is the essence of freedom. If one may choose between several alternatives, he will have a sense of freedom. This statement may be true but there are limitations on its generality which makes choice irrelevant as the essence of freedom. If one wants to survive and is confronted only with the choice of death by the firing squad or death by hanging, it is submitted that his sense of freedom is gravely impaired.

Jim's choice while enslaved is to obey the will of his master or suffer punishment. If freed, his choice is to work and earn money to buy his wife and children, do without them, or steal them and be punished if caught. The question is, Who manages available choices and whose interests are served by the extent and nature of the choices permitted? A person who can promote his own interests by defining the nature and number of choices available to others has a sense of freedom. Inevitably, to the extent that any other person must choose from among options that are incompatible with his goals, he will sense an absence of freedom. Socially created and imposed alternatives may not have the same result, however, if those who choose have been well indoctrinated with the interests of the society served by the various forms of behavior permitted.

Huck was at least partially so indoctrinated. He floated down the Mississippi to be free, and as a part of the exercise of that freedom he took Jim with him. It was more an act of defiance of law, but once on the raft he could decide to aid Jim or to change his mind and turn Jim in. When his past indoctrinations momentarily took hold, he felt a sense of freedom as he made an effort to abide by the law. In the same way, if one is the source of the law requiring his obedience and obedience to that law serves his interests, or if the source is society and the individual has been fully indoctrinated, he may well feel that obedience to law is the essence of freedom. But even so, neither theory *explains* the essence of a sense of freedom.

A close look at a sense of enhanced freedom reveals that interests of some are served under each theory. Obedience to law or choice among limited alternatives enhances one's sense of freedom if obedience or available choice eliminates obstacles to goals. For example, Jim could imagine earning money to buy his wife and children once he reached Cairo. The behavioral choice was perceived by him as eliminating an obstacle to his desire for freedom for his wife and children. He did not consider disobedience until he anticipated that even after earning money the owner of his children might refuse to sell them. Absence of obstacles to the achievement of goals optimizes one's sense of freedom. In this view, freedom is not just an abstraction with the only reality highly individualized. Nor is it just a matter of choice. There is some common ground for each person's sense of freedom. The commonality breaks down if each individual has his own peculiar goals. Conflict then is likely.

PRIMARY GOALS[3]

Extreme absence of similar goals would lead to chaos. However aggravated the discontinuity in the social condition of Western man, his situation cannot be described as chaotic, forcing the conclusion that some goals must be shared. Even Huck, Jim, his family, the two men in the boat, and the owne of Jim's children must have wanted some of the same things out of life. Harold D. Lasswell claims that the following primary goals are generally shared by Western man: (1) existence or survival, (2) physiological grati- fication, (3) love and affection, (4) respect, (5) self-respect, (6) power or control, (7) skill, (8) enlightenment, (9) prestige, (10) esthetic satis- faction, (11) excitement, (12) novelty, and perhaps many more. Obstacl to the attainment of any of these desires are likely to result in a sense of deprived freedom.

Anyone who wants to live, whether he be slave or freeman, shares the first primary goal of continued existence and survival. Threats to survival, whether in the law or in the behavior of other men, will be avoided or re- sisted by all such persons. The same can probably be said about the primar goals of physiological gratification and love and affection.

Respect is another matter. Human beings in our culture tend to want to be valued as individuals. Despite present-day love-cultism, most of us do not want or need that much feeling issuing toward us from others. Rather, to be valued for what we are provides a sense of reward and is goal achievin The black man in our society has had some difficulty in achieving this goal. He senses, accurately in all too many cases, that white men have little or no respect for him as a human being. Absence of respect affects one's view of himself. It is difficult to respect oneself if others do not. And most of us yearn to view ourselves as valuable, worthy human beings. How could Jim respect himself if he was valued for nothing other than the labor coerced from him? What must he have been imagining as he contemplated being with his wife and children while working as a free man? Certainly more than gratifying his need, say, for love and affection. He sought, surely, a self-respect, a sense of being, not permitted a slave.

Jim was looking for a way to achieve power or control over others. He believed that money had some power to get him what he wanted. But if it did not, he speculated that there still might be a way if he could find an abolitionist to help him. So he needed either some skill for which others were willing to pay or the ability to persuade an abolitionist to help him. His powers to persuade were impressive. With a few words he dissuaded Huck from turning him in to the slave hunters. He knew just what to say. Today we see increasing efforts by disadvantaged people to develop skills that will lead to more power or control over others and over their own destinies.

The quest for knowledge and wisdom is evidence of the existence of the primary goal of enlightenment. To be enlightened is to improve one's range of skills and hopefully to extend his power or control. Substantial achieve- ment of this goal, coupled with partial achievement of some of the others mentioned, permits one to begin to stand out as a special person. If it is a kind of specialness that meets with general approval, an unusually high value may be attached to the individual by others.

Jim was seeking freedom. What, in fact, did he want? Many of the things just described! For him freedom meant achieving some of these primary goals.

As one seeks freedom he may feel it is itself a primary goal. However, reflection ought to demonstrate that such a quest is instrumental in achieving a primary goal and is not a primary goal itself. To the extent that freedom is viewed as a goal, it most properly should be characterized as an instrumental goal. As one seeks freedom his behavior is best characterized as removing obstacles to the attainment of primary goals.

INSTRUMENTAL GOALS

Similarly, instrumental goals include *rationality* in problem solving; *democracy* (polyarchy, or control of leaders by nonleaders) as a political structure, to ensure that power is available to the individual; *equality,* which is subjectively sensed as a prerequisite of respect and self-respect; *security,* which is a precondition of survival and physical gratification; *progress* in the removal of obstacles; and *appropriate inclusion,* or the opportunity to act cooperatively to attain desires the individual wants for himself and others.

The individual wants those with whom he shares group membership to be rational problem solvers when they act to achieve primary goals. The means chosen, priorities established, and system devised for scheduling, coordinating, and integrating behavior—all should be rational.

Clearly, no one can achieve many of his primary goals in isolation from others. Interaction with others is obviously necessary to a condition of freedom. Although one may hope to be rational as he acts to achieve his goals, he must have a strong desire that those upon whom he depends act rationally too. One way to assure propitious associations is to choose to act jointly only with those who share one's primary goals, priorities, and notions about how to proceed. Those are the people least likely to become obstacles. Of course each must recognize the need of another individual to achieve his goals and must want that achievement for all.

Huck, who wants power and control, respect and self-respect, excitement and novelty, and who takes aim on freedom as his instrumental goal, joins with Jim the escaped slave, who immediately wants some of the more basic primary goals as well as power and control, respect and self-respect, but who probably is little interested in novelty and excitement. But Jim too desires freedom. Although there are dissimilarities in what the two want, there are certain important similarities. Huck's decision to include Jim in his adventure and Jim's decision to depend on Huck are acts of inclusion. Another instrumental goal, that the act of inclusion be appropriate, is necessary for each. Inclusion is appropriate if those depended upon can and will help one achieve his primary goals. Sometimes we find opportunities to choose associates. Sometimes the inclusion is forced on us by social circumstance. In any case, one probably constantly analyzes his interactions with others, looking for confirmation of the appropriateness of inclusion or looking for signs of deviance.[4] Huck momentarily perceived deviance in Jim's expressed intent to steal his children and acted at once to rid himself of Jim. At the moment, he had judged that to include Jim in his adventure was inappropriate. But quickly he changed his mind as Jim's appeal to Huck's sense of honor, respect, self-respect, perhaps even prestige, became more important than the deviance. And after all, the adventure could continue as they both sought freedom. Much the same thing goes on in all groups as their members constantly judge who are the "right" people and who are the "wrong" people. A correlative of appropriate inclusion is appropriate exclusion. One does not want to be bound to joint activity with others who desire other goals or who will work to his detriment as they seek their own ends. Jim did not want to remain part of a slave society. Finally, appropriate inclusion is an instrumental goal. When achieved probabilities of primary goal achievement are enhanced. When there is error, the probabilities are diminished. Blacks in our society have been trying to tell whites that to exclude them systematically from main-stream interaction is to reduce whites' chances of goal achievement.

Democracy is another instrumental goal of most Western people. No one in a group can be certain that his will is to be dominant. No one can be certain that the will of another, motivated by a conflicting self-interest, will not be dominant. Recognizing that in most groups there are few leaders and that one's chances of being a leader are slim, a method for controlling leaders so that they are not likely to act in their own self-interest and at the expense of all others becomes a goal. Effort at rational control of leaders is exerted. A condition of polyarchy is sought wherein a political structure reposes ultimate power in nonleaders for coordinating the group members' collective efforts. Most attempts at polyarchy are imperfect. On a large scale, the government of the United States resembles polyarchy. It is more nearly achieved in smaller groups. Huck seemed to be the leader on the raft, but Jim had his methods of control.

A subjective sense of equality is necessary to the achievement of primary goals of respect and self-respect. Second-class persons in any group commonly are deprived of opportunities for self-esteem by the same mechanisms that permit the first-class people to feel superior or prestigious. The prestigious individual may have little respect for the second-class person. Whether it is possible for prestigious people to rise as leaders within a poly-archic system without second-class persons, so that all people subjectively feel equal, has never been established. Is it possible for the garbage man and the governor each to view himself as the equal of the other? If polyarchy and rationality prevail, perhaps.

Achievement of the instrumental goal "security" requires effort at main-taining perceived levels of primary and instrumental goal achievement in the face of threatening change. If Jim had any idea that Huck intended to turn him in as he paddled away from the raft, he perceived the threat to his meager goal achievement. Security in what he had, a little freedom on a splinter of wood in a vast river and a lot of hope, became his goal. He acted to preserve what he had as he called out to Huck. We are all conservatives to the extent that we desire security for our levels of achievement and act accordingly.

Progress, however, is a result of desire to attain higher levels of goal achievement. Progress is change we like, whereas security is absence of change we don't like. All change is not progress: change can be viewed as regression from goals. And all stability is not security: stability can be viewed as stagnation. Progress, as a word, is properly applied by one who sees obstacles to attainment of his goals being removed by his and/or his group's efforts. To the extent that one has not fully achieved all his other goals, progress remains one of his instrumental goals. Acquiring Huck's aid to escape his slavemaster, thereby eliminating that obstacle to many of his other goals, must have been seen as progress by Jim. Furthermore, Jim's plans for more progress were implicit in his statement that he would work to earn money to buy his wife and children or steal them.

Finally, that very special instrumental goal, freedom, is sensed as one is able to do away with or avoid obstacles to appropriate inclusion, progress, security, equality, polyarchy, and rationality, which in themselves overcome obstacles to the primary goals.

LAW AND GOALS

Concerning these primary and instrumental goals, the question for the scholar is, What is the relevance of the law? Tentatively, one could hypoth-esize that because law can be used to remove some obstacles to primary goals it is itself an instrument of freedom and progress. Further, law can provide systems of operational rationality in problem solving to achieve primary goals. And law can provide opportunities for participation and control in a political system, and it may contribute to security, certainty, and stability.

The process of testing these hypotheses in order to understand the relevance of law must be preceded by some preliminary understanding of what law is. An orderly approach to that subject requires no radical or abrupt departure from the themes so far mentioned. Therefore, an easily discernibl connecting link should be relied upon. That link is the concept of justice. Books have been written about the meaning of justice, and it is almost presumptuous to offer a serious definition in a sentence or two. Nevertheless—

JUSTICE AND GOALS

Justice is primarily a value generalization constructed out of the material of primary and secondary goals. Proceeding through the instrumental goals of appropriate inclusion, progress, security, subjective equality, democracy, rationality, and freedom to the primary goals of existence or survival, physic logical gratification, love and affection, respect, and so forth, one achieves satisfying relationships and patterns of interaction. He likes them. He judges them good and right. The judgments of goodness and rightness or rectitude are socially reinforced as others in the society are satisfied with and like the same relationships and interactions. Of course, the relationships and patterns of interaction that one group likes may be incompatible with those of another group. Each group may have a different sense of justice about some things.

A good example of differing perceptions of justice in a situation is found in the novel *To Kill a Mockingbird.* Part of the plot is structured about the trial of a black man charged with assaulting a white woman. In a culture where a man's color is insignificant, the prescribed legal system would operate as though color blind. Justice would not peek at skin tone. The actors in the legal system—judges, lawyers, and jurors—would probably bear an approximate resemblance to the mix of whites and blacks in the community. But regardless of the nature of the prescribed system, this legal system was in the hands of whites for whom a man's color was very significant. The trial was taking place in a white subculture. Operationally, the legal system was white. The jurors, lawyers, and the judge, as well as all the witnesses except the accused, were white. The trial represented a mere formality, a ceremony for reconfirming the higher value of the white man and the lower value of the black. Although the evidence would, at the minimum, have convinced color-blind men that a reasonable doubt of guilt existed and, at the maximum, that the father of the girl, and not the defendant, had assaulted her, the jury found the black man guilty. The trial was a ritual, with the outcome known in advance. The evidence, only a part of the ritual transpiring, played no part in the decision. The whole process signified that whites were superior to blacks, that whites were truthful and honest, that whites were hard working and protective of their women, and that whites were in control. It further signified that blacks were inferior, that they were not to be trusted, that they lied, that they were lazy and dirty, and that they had an abiding lust for white women. Guilty! For the whites, security, prestige, self-respect, rationality, polyarchy, appropriate inclusion, survival, love and affection, and excitement and power and control were achieved or maintained by the decision. With few exceptions they sensed justice. Unless the blacks in the novel believed the same things about themselves and about the whites as the whites did, they experienced a sense of injustice. Surely, the operational legal system, the trial, and the outcome stood as obstacles to nearly all their instrumental and primary goals.

Returning to the specifics of justice and goals, the relationships and recurrent and regularized patterns of interaction achieved as a part of social structure involve not just persons with persons, but persons with things, material goods. So justice must be identified with relationships among men about persons and things that are liked. The criteria for liking and making judgments of goodness and rectitude are the primary and instrumental goals. If, for self and for others, there are obstacles to achieving primary goals, all will experience a sense of injustice. If there are no such obstacles, all will experience a sense of justice. Justice as a goal will be developed further in Chapter 3.

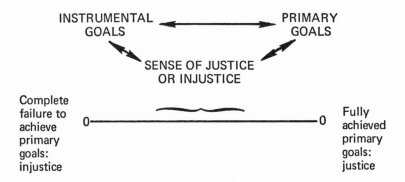

Figure 1 – 1   JUSTICE AND GOALS CONTINUUM

Justice and Goals Continuum

At one extreme on a continuum of justice (Fig. 1-1) there would be no perceived obstacles to perfect goal achievement, and thus a sense of complete justice. At the other extreme, there would be a sense of total injustice. Most men find themselves sensing mixes and combinations of justice and injustice somewhere between the extremes.

Following this line of reasoning, it can be concluded that justice is a sense of achievement of desired order among persons and with things. Therefore, it is on a different level of goals than the primary and instrumental goals. It arises out of the process of evaluating the relationship of primary and instrumental goals.

Huck's confused feelings upon returning to the raft are excellent examples of mixes and combinations of senses of justice and injustice. To the extent that he wanted freedom for Jim and acted to preserve it for the moment, he no doubt sensed justice in his behavior. But to the extent that the established order had furnished him with security to survive, to have a roof over his head and occasionally a full stomach, he knew when he lied to the slave hunters that he had betrayed those who furnished him with these things and depended upon his support in return.

Contemporary dramatists and novelists tend to focus more on clear-cut injustice than on the mixes and combinations. In real life, justice and injustice are seldom so clear-cut. But one can experience the mix for himself even in reading *To Kill a Mockingbird* if he identifies completely with neither the whites nor the blacks. The certainty that justice prevailed perceptively diminishes as one who originally identified with the whites allows himself to want and feel as the blacks did. With each increment of black perspective, the confusion grows until the black perspective dominates. From then on, each increment reduces the confusion and increases the certainty that injustice was done.

Imagine this real-life situation: a young marine in Vietnam was flying in one of a large fleet of helicopters with his buddies toward the DMZ. Their assignment was to load all the inhabitants of a small village onto the helicopters and take them to a relocation center. There was only one obstacle. An eighty-year-old man, who feared flying, resisted the young marine's efforts to put him on the helicopter. Certainly, the old man could have been carried to the machine and thrown aboard. But the commanding officer was ordering "hurry." Choppers whirled into the air. "Hurry!" The old man was crying, screaming, resisting. The young man found a solution. He shot the old man several times in the face, left him for dead, and leaped aboard.

He was met with great rejoicing and backslapping. He was being congratulated for his "kill." He was something special. A feeling of satisfaction enveloped him. He had done the right thing. He was respected. He respected himself. The mission was a success. He had contributed to it in a way no one else had. There was a sense of justice in his heart.

After he was discharged, the young marine returned to his studies, under the G.I. Bill. At the university his feelings about the incident in Vietnam began to change. Before long his memory of it left him in misery. What had happened to that sense of justice? Why had a strong sense of his act as unjust gradually developed? For a time his feelings about the event were mixed and confusing to him. Eventually he was certain that his act was unjust.

His own analysis of the transformation relied heavily on the relationship of justice to primary and instrumental goals. As a recruit at boot camp, he constantly heard Vietnamese referred to as gooks, zips, slants. Never once did anyone refer to them as human beings. He was taught that his basic function was to kill the enemy—the Vietnamese. There was no difference between Vietnamese, North and South. None could be trusted: so he was told. It was made clear to him that his and his buddies' survival depended on his becoming a killer of gooks. Inclusion was appropriate only for marines. Nothing that he saw in Vietnam seemed to contradict this indoctrination. When he killed, he removed an obstacle to survival. His buddies applauded. To kill was rational. . . progress . . . just.

The mood was different at the university. Fellow students questioned the wisdom of intervention in Vietnam. There was talk about the Vietnamese "people," the "human" suffering and tragedy, the needless deaths of "children," "women," and "old men," and the desires of Vietnamese people to be left alone to tend their fields, feed their families, and develop the skills to exercise power and control over their own lives. Some suggested that the war was an irrational way to save the Vietnamese people or to promote progress. Others rejected as contemptuous the weekly body count, which everyone suspected included dead children, old men, and pigs. Still others suggested that no American interest was served by the deaths of these human beings.

As the young student began to accept some of these beliefs, he often vacillated in his judgment about "the act." It was right to protect his buddies, but it was wrong needlessly to take the life of a human who posed them no threat. He was at a stage of disturbing mixes and combinations of senses of justice and injustice.

As his marine indoctrination slipped into an increasingly distant past, he came to believe that it is not rational to view as enemy the people you are supposed to be helping. It was irrational to function as a killer of noncombatant old men who wanted only to live free of the terror of bombs, bullets, and infernal machines. Such behavior eliminated no obstacles to his goals, the goals of his fellow marines, or the goals of his fellow Americans. The old man wanted only what the young man wanted—to stay alive. Indeed, could not the relocation mission have been viewed as an effort to remove the old man from the war zone and to save his life? Did the old man's irrational failure to cooperate justify his death? Hardly. Was his buddies' security threatened? He came to think not. The act was unjust. In *To Kill A Mockingbird* whites sensed that an event was just. Blacks sensed injustice in the same event. The young marine turned student, first sensed justice, later injustice, in an act. Huckleberry Finn experienced a more common mix of senses of justice and injustice.

Order or Social Structure

The goal of justice can be used as a bridge in the quest for the relevance of primary goals, instrumental goals, and law. If, using instrumental and primary goal achievement as criteria, the individual can judge that he likes the relationships among persons and things available to him, he will have a sense of rectitude, a sense of justice about the order he sees or participates in. Therefore, as one actively works for justice, he attempts to control relationships and to regularize patterns of interaction. He attempts to establish order, which is conducive to justice.

Order can be defined as recurrent and regularized interaction among two or more people. This is also the definition of social structure. Order is neutral. Existing order is just only to the extent that it is perceived as facilitating attainment of desires. It is unjust to the extent that it blocks goal achievement.

Law and Order

"Order" in the call for law and order means creating, maintaining, and implementing relationships the individual likes. In this context, law is a tool for creating, maintaining, and implementing recurrent and regularized interactions which may facilitate or block primary and instrumental goal achievement and the achievement of justice. Thus the presence or absence of justice depends upon the nature of order, which, in part at least, may depend upon law.

Law, Order, and Freedom

Consider now three slogans: "Obedience to law is freedom." "Law is necessary to the existence of freedom." "Law impinges on freedom." The first and third should appear too limited to be meaningful statements. Obedience to law that maintains an order that contains obstacles to the attainment of desires will not promote a sense of freedom or justice. However, law may create an order that eliminates obstacles, thereby promoting a sense of freedom and justice.

About the second slogan we must ask, Is law necessary to the existence of freedom? An answer can be developed only when one has some understanding of the nature, functions, and limitations of law—which can be understood only in social context. Herman Melville proposed a simple relationship between law, order, and freedom.

The allusion to the waifs and waif-poles in the last chapter but one, necessitates some account of the laws and regulations of the whale fishery, of which the waif may be deemed the grand symbol and badge.

It frequently happens that when several ships are cruising in company, a whale may be struck by one vessel, then escape, and be finally killed and captured by another vessel, and herein are indirectly comprised many minor contingencies, all partaking of this one grand feature. For example—after a weary and perilous chase and capture of a whale, the body may get loose from the ship by reason of a violent storm; and drifting far away to leeward, be retaken by a second whaler, who, in a calm, snugly tows it alongside, without risk of life or line. Thus the most vexatious and violent disputes would often arise between the fishermen, were there not some written or unwritten universal, undisputed law applicable to all cases.

Perhaps the only formal whaling code authorized by legislative enactment was that of Holland. It was decreed by the States-General in A.D. 1695. But though no other nation has ever had any written whaling law, yet the American fishermen have been their own legislators and lawyers in this matter. They have provided a system which for terse comprehensiveness surpasses Justinian's Pandects and the by-laws of the Chinese Society for the Suppression of Meddling with other People's Business. Yes; these laws might be engraven on a Queen Anne's farthing, or the barb of a harpoon, and worn round the neck, so small are they.

I. A Fast-Fish belongs to the party fast to it.

II. A Loose-Fish is fair game for anybody who can soonest catch it. But what plays the mischief with this masterly code is the admirable brevity of it, which necessitates a vast volume of commentaries to expound it.

First: What is a Fast-Fish? Alive or dead a fish is technically fast, when it is connected with an occupied ship or boat, by any medium at all controllable by the occupant or occupants—a mast, an oar, a nine-inch cable, a telegraph wire, or a strand of cobweb, it is all the same. Likewise a fish is technically fast when it bears a waif, or any other recognized symbol of possession; so long as the party waifing it plainly evince their ability at any time to take it alongside, as well as their intention so to do.

These are scientific commentaries; but the commentaries of the whalemen themselves sometimes consist in hard words and harder knocks—the Coke-upon-Littleton of the fist. True, among the more upright and honorable whalemen allowances are always made for peculiar cases, where it would be an outrageous moral injustice for one party to claim possession of a whale previously chased or killed by another party. But others are by no means so scrupulous.

Some fifty years ago there was a curious case of whale-trover litigated in England, wherein the plaintiffs set forth that after a hard chase of a whale in the Northern seas; and when indeed they (the plaintiffs) had succeeded in harpooning the fish; they were at last, through peril of their lives, obliged to forsake not only their lines, but their boat itself. Ultimately the defendants (the crew of another ship) came up with the whale, struck, killed seized, and finally appropriated it before the very eyes of the plaintiffs. And when those defendants were remonstrated with their captain snapped his fingers in the plaintiffs' teeth, and assured them that by way of doxology to the deed he had done, he would not retain their line, harpoons, and boat which had remained attached to the whale at the time of the seizure. Where fore the plaintiffs now sued for the recovery of the value of their whale, line, harpoons, and boat.

Mr. Erskine was counsel for the defendants; Lord Ellenborough was the judge. In the course of the defense, the witty Erskine went on to illustrate his position, by alluding to a recent crim. con. case, wherein a gentleman, after in vain trying to bridle his wife's viciousness, had at last abandoned her upon the seas of life; but in the course of years, repenting the step, he instituted an action to recover possession of her. He then proceeded to say that, though the gentleman had originally harpooned the lady, and at once had her fast, and only by reason of the great stress of her plunging viciousness, had at last abandoned her; yet abandon her he did, so that she became a loose-fish; and therefore when a subsequent gentleman re-harpooned her, the lady then became that subsequent gentleman's property, along with whatever harpoon might have been found sticking in her.

Now in the present case Erskine contended that the examples of the whale and the lady were reciprocally illustrative of each other.

These pleadings, and the counter-pleadings, being duly heard, the very learned judge in set terms decided, to wit—That as for the boat, he awarded it to the plaintiffs, because they had merely abandoned it to save their lives; but that with regard to the controverted whale harpoons, and line the belonged to the defendant; the whale, because it was a Loose-Fish at the time of the final capture; and the harpoons and line because when the fish made off with them, it (the fish) acquired a property in those articles; and hence anybody who afterwards took the fish had a right to them. Now the plaintiffs afterwards took the fish; ergo, the aforesaid articles were theirs.

A common man looking at this decision of the very learned judge might possibly object to it. But ploughed up to the primary rock of the matter, the two great principles laid down in the twin whaling laws previously quoted, and applied and elucidated by Lord Ellenborough in the above cited case; these two laws touching Fast-Fish and Loose-Fish, I say, will, on reflection, be found the fundamentals of all human jurisprudence; for not withstanding its complicated tracery of sculpture, the Temple of the Law, like the Temple of the Philistines, has but two props to stand on.

Is it not a saying in everyone's mouth. Possession is half of the law: that is, regardless of how the thing came into possession? But often possession is the whole of the law. What are the sinews and souls of Russian serfs and Republican slaves but Fast-Fish, whereof possession is the whole of the law? What to the rapacious landlord is the widow's last mite but a Fast-Fish? What is yonder undetected villain's marble mansion with a door-plate for a waif; what is that but a Fast-Fish? What is the ruinous discount which Mordecai, the broker, gets from poor Woebegone, the bankrupt, on a loan to keep Woebegone's family from starvation; what is that ruinous discount but a Fast-Fish? What is the Archbishop of Savesoul's income £100,000 but a Fast-fish? What are the Duke of Dunder's hereditary towns and hamlets but a Fast-Fish? What to that redoubted harpooneer, John Bull, is poor Ireland, but a Fast-Fish? What to that apostolic lancer, Brother Jonathan, is Texas but a Fast-Fish? And concerning all these, is not Possession the whole of the law?

But if the doctrine of Fast-Fish be pretty generally applicable, the kindred doctrine of Loose-Fish is still more widely so. That is internationally and universally applicable.

What was America in 1492 but a Loose-Fish, in which Columbus struck the Spanish standard by way of waifing it for his royal master and mistress? What was Poland to the Czar? What Greece to the Turk? What India to England? What at last will Mexico be to the United States? All Loose-Fish.

What are the Rights of Man and the Liberties of the World but Loose-Fish? What all men's minds and opinions but Loose-Fish? What to the ostentatious smuggling verbalists are the thoughts of thinkers but Loose-Fish? What is the great globe itself but a Loose-Fish! And what are you, reader, but a Loose-Fish and a Fast-Fish, too?[5]

Though it is appealing to reduce notions of law, order, and freedom to such simplistics, they are likely to become slogans and, as such, substitutes for thought. Thought is then absent—and ability to know and understand the complexities of reality is stunted. It is better to be adrift in a sea of ambiguity and uncertainty than on a shore of over simplification.

Research and knowledge are best promoted in an uncertain sea, and the hypotheses stated under "Law and Order" in this chapter should continue to be an important, more distant, less accessible, but ultimately more rewarding shore. Figure 1–2 enlarges upon the justice-goals continuum presented in Figure 1–1.

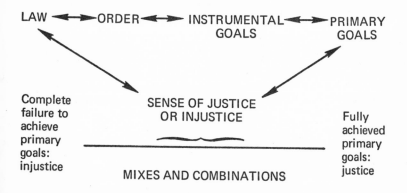

Figure 1 – 2   JUSTICE, GOALS, AND LAW AND
ORDER CONTINUUM

NOTES

1. Mark Twain, *Huckleberry Finn* (New York: Harper & Brothers, 1918), Chap. XVI.

2. Kenneth M. Stamp, *The Causes of the Civil War* (Englewood Cliffs, N. J.: Prentice-Hall, 1959).

3. The following discussion is based on concepts of primary and instrumental goals propounded by Harold D. Lasswell in *Power and Personality* (New York: Norton, 1948).

4. Kai T. Erikson's *The Wayward Puritans: A Study in the Sociology of Deviance* (New York: Wiley, 1966) is a very interesting study of how the Puritans looked for, found, and defined deviance. The author's hypothesis is that the amount of deviance is constant throughout time within a given group and that the search for deviance helps the group to define itself and its goals. He believes that groups need deviance. Essentially, the same point will be made later in this work, when the relationship between conflict and social structure is explored.

5. Herman Melville, *Moby Dick; or The Whale* (Chicago: Encyclopedia Britannica, Great Books of the Western World, 1952), Chap. 29, pp. 292–295, as cited by Ephraim London, ed., *The World of Law,* vol. II, *The Law as Literature* (New York: Simon & Schuster, 1970), pp. 599-602.)

2

SOCIAL STRUCTURE

FUNCTIONAL EXIGENCIES

Each of us has primary and instrumental goals, and for each there are obstacles. Strain is a broad characterization for the resulting senses of injustice and freedom deprivation and their accompanying emotional and intellectual discomfort. Some behavior intended to relieve the strain may result. Whatever its form, such behavior can be characterized as reaction to strain. The premise is that individuals react to the strain that results from the existence of obstacles to the achievement of their desires. A further premise is that individuals participate in the functioning of a social system and that the functional exigencies of the social system include modes of economic, political, integrative, and cultural activity. The economic function includes modes of production, exchange, and consumption of goods. The political function includes the modes of coordinating and controlling a social system's collective actions. This usually is thought to be done by the state. The integrative function includes modes of creating, maintaining, and implementing norms governing interactions among individuals and among organizations or units in a social system. The cultural function includes modes of creating and maintaining cultural values. This four-part classification of modes of behavior in a social system serves convenience, but one must be cautioned that any specific individual behavior may be a part of one, two, three, or all four modes. The same may be said for

---

The elements of social structure discussed in this chapter are drawn from Neil J. Smelser, *The Sociology of Economic Life,* Englewood Cliffs, N. J., Prentice-Hall (1963). Herein, application of the elements is made to "legal life."

recurrent and regularized interactions of two or more people—that is, social structure. Figure 2-1 represents a summary of this paragraph.

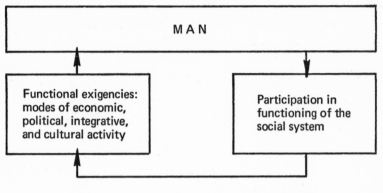

Figure 2 – 1   FUNCTIONAL EXIGENCIES

ROLES

People usually engage in organized clusters of activities. These activities are more or less common behavior for them in each of their roles—for example, as a father or mother, business person, club member, and citizen. The organized clusters of activities include interactions with various parts of their environment, which aid in identifying the various roles they are playing. Their interactions with physical, social, and cultural aspects of their environment amount to their participation in the functional exigencies which enable their social system to endure. They affect the functioning of their social system environment which has had its effect on them by supplying them with values, norms, and sanctions, which tend to structure and regulate their organized clusters of activities, in other words, to define the nature of their various roles. The social system thereby induces conformity of behavior and certain expectations while the individual participates in the social system.

The theory of the individual's participation in his social system described so far is summarized in Figure 2-2.

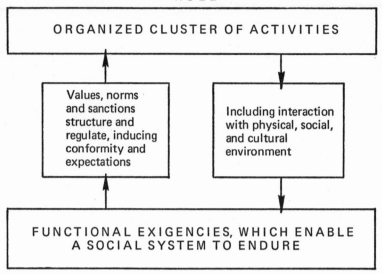

Figure 2 – 2   ROLE

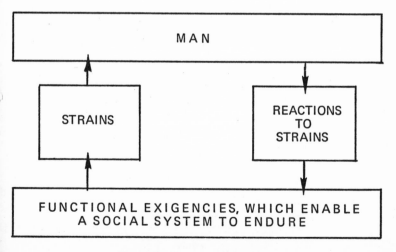

Figure 2 – 3   STRAINS

STRAINS AND REACTIONS

The nature of the social system's functional exigencies acting on the individual never perfectly serve him by removing all obstacles to the achievement of his desires. They will do so only imperfectly and incomplete

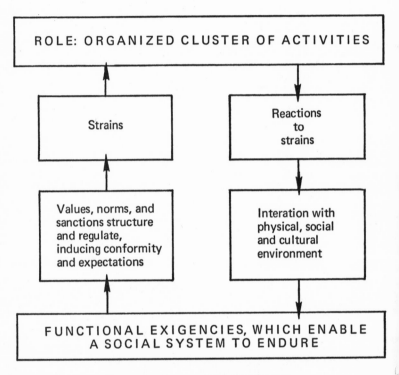

Figure 2 – 4   ROLE STRAINS

and may even contribute to the existence of such obstacles. Thus they are a source of both satisfaction and strains. Figure 2-3 emphasizes strains and Figure 2-4 integrates the previous models.

SOCIAL STRUCTURE AND CONTROL

Because they impose values, norms, and sanctions upon the individual, the classified modes of behavior described as functional exigencies tend to promote recurrent and regularized behavior interactions. Social control and social structure relationships depicted in Figure 2-5 and Figure 2-6 integrate these concepts with the previous models.

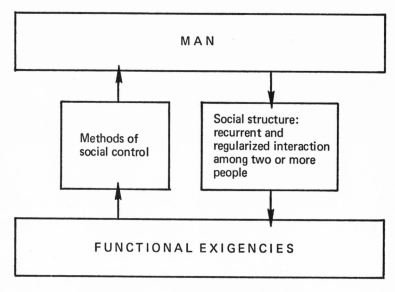

Figure 2 – 5   SOCIAL STRUCTURE

ATTITUDINAL AND BEHAVIORAL CHANGE

The values, norms, and sanctions of a social system usually only imperfectly and incompletely remove obstacles because they are often ambiguous, sometimes are in conflict, and are replete with discrepancies. Huckleberry Finn was one of their victims. So, in addition to any direct deprivations caused, social complexity results in all kinds of indirect deprivations for the individual. His social system's order is defective: It falls short of instrumental and primary goal achievement. He senses some absence of freedom, progress, security, appropriate inclusion, rationality, and equality with resulting obstacles to his primary desires. He senses mixes and combinations of injustice. He feels strains. Huck was acutely aware of them. Specifically, he will experience conflicts of values, discrepancies between his expectations and the actual social situation, conflicts among his roles, and ambiguities in his role expectations.

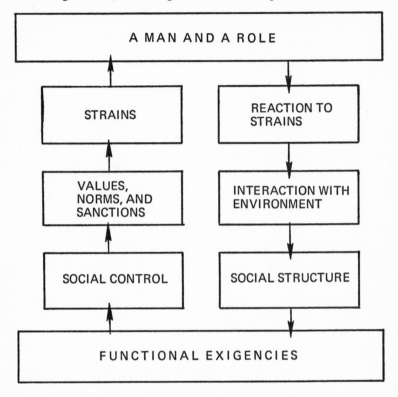

Figure 2 – 6   ROLE AND SOCIAL STRUCTURE

Reaction takes two basic forms, attitudinal and behavioral. Attitudinally a man's morale may be affected and his beliefs and ideologies may change. For example, in order to relieve strain he may devise an ideological fiction about the rugged individualism of businessmen. He may subscribe to a protestant ethic that equates reward with excellence and deprivations with inferiority. In one case, he generates a fiction to ease his strain. By the other, he has generated an ideological belief as a moral justification of existing arrangements—for example, by espousing an ideological belief in the social responsibility of businessmen. Behaviorally a vast array of changes may accompany attitude changes. A man's behavior may become deviant. He may be a chronic absentee or alcoholic. Or he may turn to some form of crime or to suicide. Or he may exert great effort at rational calculation and control of his environment.

Figure 2-7 represents the relationship of the consequences of the imbalances and discontinuities of social control to attitudinal and behavioral change.[1] Figure 2-8 integrates all the models.

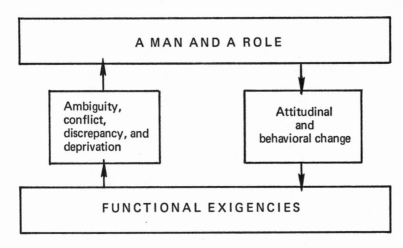

Figure 2 – 7   ROLE AND BEHAVIOR

Figure 2-8 is deceptive if it is misread. For example, social structure as cause seems remote from attitudinal and behavioral change as effect. This chart displays only the parts of a dissected organism, not the organism alive and functioning. The modes of the functional exigencies are social structure, including the role of the individual. One may read the chart to say that attitudinal and behavioral change affects social structure; but one may also read the chart to say that social structure affects attitudinal and behavioral change. A more complex version of this chart will be found in Chapter 7.

LAW AND SOCIAL ENGINEERING

Applying this model to the area of law, one can see values, norms, and sanctions (including law) structuring and regulating as well as inducing conformity and expectations—one can see them as tools in the construction of order for the purpose of achieving instrumental and primary goals. One can also see these goals imperfectly achieved or even impaired by the established order, resulting in mixed senses of justice, injustice, and strain.

In reaction to the strain, there are four common types of behavior: Law may be broken; one may fantasize about the law and the social condition; one may exert effort at preserving an existing law; and one may want to change an existing law. Where one rationally calculates the social condition

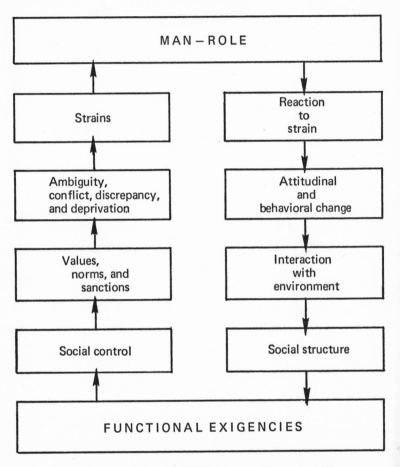

Figure 2 – 8   MAN AND HIS ENVIRONMENT

and his place in it, and thereafter makes an effort to control the functioning of the social structure for better goal achievement by contributing to the elimination of obstacles such as waste and frictions resulting from ambiguities, conflict, discrepancy, and deprivations, he is acting as a social engineer.

Roscoe Pound explained his understanding of the law and goal achievement. He called it social engineering.

For the purpose of understanding the law of today, I am content with a picture of satisfying as much of the whole body of human wants as we may with the least sacrifice. I am content to think of law as a social institution to satisfy social wants—the claims and demands and expectations involved in the existence of civilized society—by giving effect to as much as we may with the least sacrifice, so far as such wants may be satisfied or such claims given effect by an ordering of human conduct through politically organized society. For the present purposes, I am content to see in legal history the record of a continually wide recognizing and satisfying of human wants or desires through social control; a more embracing and more effective securing of social interests; a continually more complete and effective elimination of waste and precluding of friction in human enjoyment of the goods of existence—in short, a continually more efficacious social engineering.[2]

As a social engineer, one may employ the law as a tool for constructing, maintaining, and implementing recurrent and regularized interactions which facilitate elimination of obstacles to attainment of desires. But one can do this only when he knows what law is, what it does, and what it can not do. The hypotheses about law already expressed may have added to them the element of the social engineer, in which case they would read as follows: Law can be used as an instrument of social engineering to remove some obstacles to primary goals, thereby promoting freedom and progress. The social engineer attempts to use law to provide systems of operational rationality wherein decision techniques, appropriate to the circumstances and goals, aid in problem solving. Law can be used by the social engineer to provide opportunities for participation and control in a political system. The law may be used as an instrument of social engineering to contribute to social conditions promoting democracy and appropriate inclusion. The social engineer may use law to promote security, certainty, and stability. Though demonstrations of these statements follow, there is no question about the need for much research in this fertile area.

NOTES

1. This model represents attitudinal and behavioral change as concurrent only for convenience. Which comes first is an important problem in the law. Some law will probably never evoke behavioral change because the behavior is dependent on a contradictory attitude. Yet an approach to changing attitude by employing law tools includes effort to legislate new

behavior with the hope that new attitudes compatible with enforced behavior will develop. Some studies have demonstrated that the latter is successful in certain cases. See Daryl J. Bem, *Beliefs, Attitudes and Human Affairs* (Belmont, Calif.: Brooks/Cole, 1970).

2. Roscoe Pound, *An Introduction to the Philosophy of Law* (New Haven, Conn.: Yale University Press, 1961), p. 47.

3

LEGAL SYSTEMS

So far, primary and instrumental goals have been discussed in relation to concepts of justice, law, and order. And there has been a brief description of the social context within which one employing law tools is cast in the role of a social engineer. The next hypothesis is that law is a powerful social tool for the attainment of justice and instrumental and primary goals, and that rational use of this tool requires knowledge of its nature, functions, and limitations. Further, it is hypothesized that law can be used by the individual to change social structure in order to relieve strain and senses of injustice. Finally, each individual in whom attitudinal and behavioral changes are evoked by the strains of social control is an incipient social engineer. He may employ law as a tool to create, maintain, and implement recurrent regularized interactions that facilitate goal achievement.

PRECONDITIONS OF A LEGAL SYSTEM[1]

The Group

Law is not a tool for the person effectively isolated from his fellow man. (One may be in proximity to others but associate with them in no way.) However, when he associates with one or more others, the individual probably does so to help satisfy some of his basic desires. They associate with him for the same reason. A recognizable group, not a mere collection of people in proximity, is formed when there is joint effort toward the achievement of common goals. It takes only two or more people developing recurrent and regularized goal-oriented behavior for the model depicted in

Figure 2-8 to come into existence. The regular behavior has the effect of social control with its own values, norms, and sanctions. The first precondition of a legal system exists: a group.

It must be emphasized at this point that primary goal achievement requires instrumental goal achievement and that instrumental goal achieveme requires a group with social structure. This inevitability can be diagramme as follows:

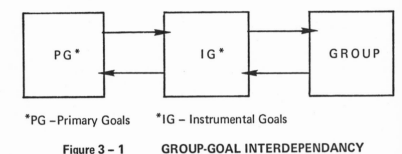

*PG –Primary Goals   *IG – Instrumental Goals

Figure 3 – 1   GROUP-GOAL INTERDEPENDANCY

Divergence of Urges

Depending upon the number in and complexity of the group, the structure and regulation of behavior inducing conformity and certain expectations may not appear fully adequate to each member in the fulfillment of his goals. The group's priorities of goals may not match his. Further, ambiguities in role expectations and actual special situations and conflicts of values will create strains in him and divergence of urges among members of the group. Under the circumstances, a member may see the behavior of another, others, or the whole group deviating from his goals, which he felt he held in common with them. The group, others, or another may regard his behavior as deviant. The perceived deviant or evasive behavior may be tolerable, or an ideology may grow within the group justifying some forms of deviance. In such instances, the divergence of urges probably presents no immediate trouble for the group or long-term impediments to the achievement of its goals. But with the existence of divergence of urges within the group, the second precondition of a legal system is established.

Claims

When divergency of urges among individuals within the group or among individuals and the group that cannot be tolerated by those affected finally appear, the group is in danger of destruction because the important divergencies are perceived as obstacles to instrumental and primary goals. Divergent members may leave the group and seek attainment of their desires elsewhere. They may ease strain subjectively by developing fictions to replace reality. They may resort to absenteeism or alcoholism to escape reality. In each case, the effectiveness of the group in achieving its goals is probably impaired. But when those in conflict among themselves or with the group face the realities of the existence of the conflict and its nature and wish still to seek attainment of their desires within the group, then they or the group may demand of the other that their claims and expectations be recognized and protected by resolving conflicts in their favor. The third precondition for the existence of a legal system then exists: a claim.

Figure 3-2 builds on Figure 3-1, adding the preconditions of a legal system representing how naturally they tend to evolve.

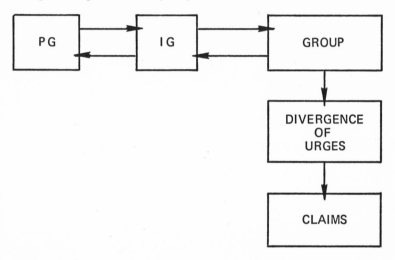

Figure 3 –2   GOALS AND THE PRECONDITIONS OF LAW

CONDITIONS OF A LEGAL SYSTEM

"Must" and Supremacy

How is the group to choose between conflicting claims arising out of divergence of urges? Who is to do the choosing? No legal system can exist if there is no fundamental mechanism for resolving conflicts. What if one of the parties refuses to submit to the conflict-resolution mechanism? How can the group enforce a decision? On whose behalf does the mechanism purport to operate? What criteria are used to resolve disputes? It is not sufficient to establish procedures if disputants can successfully challenge the power of those charged with making such decisions. If the power to make or to enforce the decision is uncertain, because it is successfully challenged then no legal system can exist. A necessity of a legal system is that it can successfully resist challenges. Two conditions are then present: a "must" element and a "supremacy" element.

The must condition of a legal system consists of the ability to employ physical or psychological coercion so that the parties to a claim-conflict feel they "must" abide by the solution developed by the decision maker. Closely related is the supremacy condition, which simply means that any challenge to the appropriateness of the group's decision machinery and personnel will fail and that thereby the group's institution maintains its supremacy.

In our state legal systems, if one against whom a claim is laid chooses not to participate in the resolution of the conflict, he is taken care of in one of several ways. If the case concerns a breach of contract, for example, the defendant's refusal to appear will not prevent a court from acting. A default judgment will be entered against him. If the defendant has been accused of a crime, the solution is not as simple because our laws do not permit default convictions. Law enforcement officers may search the world to find the reluctant defendant and return him to the system for his day in court.

In the contract case, once a decision is made, say, against the defendant, a sheriff will be ordered to seize his property, convert it to cash and pay the judgment if he does not voluntarily pay up. A criminal conviction results in some form of punishment. All demonstrate that challenges are overcome and that decisions stick.

Wholeness

Another element of a legal system can be characterized as the "wholeness" condition. That is, the solutions to claims-conflicts are purportedly made on behalf of the whole group. The methods and persons prescribed by the group for resolving conflict are established in order to remove the obstacles to the group's ability to achieve its goals and thereby remove the obstacles to the attainment of individual desires, which were the bases for group formation in the first place.

In the experience of most men with the legal systems of most groups, actions sometimes seem to benefit only a few or only the officials. What seems to be may be true, and yet there is a legal system because officials need only purport to be acting for the whole group as they act for themselves. The pretense is necessary to preserve some sense of legitimacy. After all, the only excuse for the existence of a legal system is in its service to the group whose members quest after instrumental and primary goals.

In a recent movie, a young man returns from Europe to his homeland, now ruled by a dictator with whom he is acquainted. The young man sees that many homes have been destroyed in the central city and that a ceremonial parade ground has been built in their place. The dictator also has constructed a huge and costly palace. The young man questions him about his responsibility to ensure that the displaced people are properly housed. The dictator replies that he has built a palace for the people.

Recognized Officialdom

The fourth and final element of a legal system has been alluded to in the discussion of the first three. The decision maker recognized by the group as acting according to duties and procedures conferred upon or assumed by him makes decisions affecting the welfare of the whole group, purportedly on behalf of the group, and successfully repels all challenges that he may not so act, including effective forced compliance with his decisions. The "recognized officialdom" condition of a legal system is thus characterized and must be present.

Those subject to the decisions and acts of the official need not like him or his deeds, but he is nevertheless recognized as the one who does decide. The blacks in *To Kill a Mockingbird* recognized the judge and jurors as officials. Undoubtedly, the decision could have been rationalized as in the best interests of blacks as well as whites given the color-conscious social setting and the paternalistic attitude of whites toward blacks. Also, under the circumstances, no challenge of the jury, the court, or their decision was likely to prevail. They may have made a mistake, but they had authority. An appellate court review can correct a mistake without challenging the authority, but the story never got that far. The convicted black's mistrust of the system caused him to try to escape and he was shot to death.

Perhaps Jim had successfully challenged authority in his escape from slavery. His initial success was giving him ideas for further challenges. But there were hunters resisting his challenge. They were looking for him—or others like him.

AUTHORITY

The four conditions of a legal system are also the elements of authority. Authority is necessary to two of a society's four functional exigencies. Some authority is necessary to coordinate and control collective actions, and in many instances it is necessary to govern interactions among individuals and subgroups. To the extent that such political and integrative behavior may be found in economic and cultural modes of behavior, authority may also be present in those functional exigencies. Some behavior in all these areas can result because of controls other than authority. Nonlaw social norms and customs, a price system, nonauthoritative coercion, persuasion, and bargaining can be examples. Not unimportant are spontaneous controls[2] in which the individual may evoke unintentional and unplanned behavior in others as he acts, the cumulative effect of which can contain some elements of all four functional exigencies.

Although social control mechanisms other than law exist, no group functions for long, given the presence of preconditions of a legal system, without the exercise of some authority. Authority is therefore necessary to a group' continued survival. The elements of authority are the identical conditions of a legal system. Therefore, no group long survives without a legal system. Legal systems are necessary.

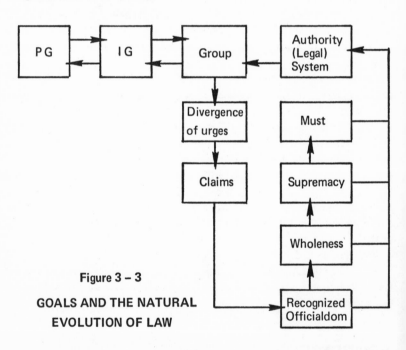

Figure 3 – 3

GOALS AND THE NATURAL
EVOLUTION OF LAW

Figure 3-3 expands upon the diagram presented in Figure 3-2. The authority system, which also is nearly inevitable, must be placed in its proper position.

To relate Figure 3-3 to justice, one must compare it with Figures 1-1 and 1-2. Figure 1-1 demonstrates how a sense of justice or injustice is a product of goal achievement or failure. Figure 1-2 demonstrates that justice is a product of goal achievement or failure of law and order. A refinement in our treatment of the source of a sense of justice or injustice is now possible. In Figure 3–4, perceived goal achievement is represented as the source of a sense of justice and the legal system as the apparent source of a sense of justice. Only if the legal system affects perceptions of goal achievement is justice or injustice felt. Nothing in the legal system, by itself, can give rise to a sense of justice, However, social indoctrination causes one to believe that justice is directly derived from the operation of a legal system. Also represented in Figure 3–4 is justice preceding the law. The desire to sense justice in events may cause people to look to law as an instrument to control these events. To the degree that a sense of justice or injustice precedes the existence and function of a legal system in its service, a legal system cannot be the source of that sense. Here justice is depicted as a product of primary and instrumental goals and as a goal-prodding behavior characterized as the functional exigencies' political and integrative modes.

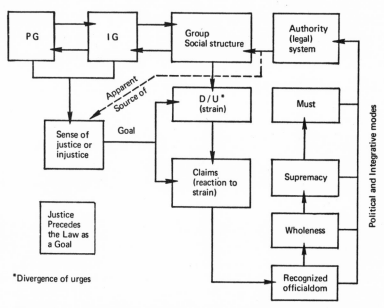

Figure 3 – 4 THE RELATIONSHIP OF GOALS, JUSTICE AND LAW

The model in Figure 3–4 was built from simple beginnings. In real-life situations there are few simple beginnings. For most people in most groups the starting point in this model is the group into which they are born. The group supplies the primary and instrumental goals, the senses of justice and injustice, and the legal system. Researchers can use this model to generate hypotheses for testing and analysis.

POWER

There are almost as many theories and definitions of the nature of power as there are authors who choose to write about the subject. No claim is made that the treatment of power here is superior to any other analysis of power. For the purposes of this discussion, power is considered as several "things": authority, force, persuasion, and influence.[3]

Authority

The official's power base for affecting the quality of life is authority. From that base he may act in ways that remove or create obstacles to the achievement of others' primary and instrumental goals. He is a group's most visible problem solver—or problem maker. But the analysis here of the social context within which all members of a group act, demonstrates, it is admitted, that each individual makes some contribution to the quality of life. He helps remove or create obstacles to the achievement of goals as he reacts to the strains caused by his social system. He is only a less visible problem solver or maker. He too must have some power base. Exactly what the base is may vary from person to person, depending for the moment on his role and the relevant group or subgroup to which he belongs. A father may possess an authority base in the family. The same may be said of an executive in a business corporation, or the president of a club.

Force

The power base of the individual other than a recognized group official will vary in its elements. Coercive power may exist in physical, psychological or monetary form for almost anybody. If it cannot be successfully resisted or challenged by a person subject to it, then he possesses two elements of power—the must element and the supremacy element. He may exert such power exclusively for his own benefit, or on behalf of others, or purportedly on behalf of the whole group. But the wholeness element of authority is not clearly present and the recognized officialdom element is absent. To differentiate it from an authority base, he can be said to occupy a power base of force. Anyone with a supremacy element in any given situation has power. Force is a subset of power.

Influence

In achieving some end a recognized official may choose not to rely on the "must" element of his authority. It may be that he has no authority to do what he undertakes on behalf of the group. Or he may be using his position to give special powei to his attempts at promoting his own interests, the interests of another individual, or the interests of a subgroup. President Kennedy, using the position of his office, may have succeeded in causing steel prices to be rolled back even though he had no authority to require them to be rolled back for the welfare of the country. Or a policeman may convince a prosecutor not to bring charges against a friend's son only to the benefit of that friend. The essence of the behavior in each case is persuasion with the special compelling attribute that it is being done by an official, enhancing the probabilities that resistance to the act is less likely to exist or is more easily overcome. If one is successful, he can be said to have influence. Influence has two elements: supremacy and recognized officialdom. The wholeness element may or may not be present depending upon who purportedly is being benefited.

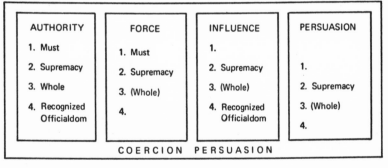

AUTHORITY	FORCE	INFLUENCE	PERSUASION
1. Must	1. Must	1.	
2. Supremacy	2. Supremacy	2. Supremacy	1.
3. Whole	3. (Whole)	3. (Whole)	2. Supremacy
4. Recognized Officialdom	4.	4. Recognized Officialdom	3. (Whole)
			4.

COERCION   PERSUASION

Figure 3 – 5   POWER

Persuasion

A person other than a recognized official who successfully seeks extra-authoritative results from an act of intercession by an official on his or another's behalf may feel that he has influence, but it is derivative or vicarious influence more appropriately classified in a different power base: persuasion. The persuasion power base is occupied by most people most of the time in most of their roles in most groups. Words and acts are used in persuading and bargaining. Words and acts are employed to reach reason or emotion and induce behavior. Purely behavioral persuasion evokes emulation if it is successful. Successful verbal persuasion overcomes alternative ways of acting in the minds of those approached. One may attempt to control the behavior and attitudes of others by persuasion, but he almost always does so in an arena of competing ideas and other persuasive behavior. He can be said to have the power of persuasion only if his ideas prevail over ideas that challenge his. In other words, the supremacy element must be present. However, no other element need be present. Wholeness as an element may or may not be present. Figure 3-5 compares the four fundamental power bases.[4]

If authority's must element is the proper place of all coercion in a group, then employment of coercion by an individual to achieve his goals is likely to be viewed as deviant behavior. A great deal of the exercise of force is defined by authority systems as illegitimate and criminal or at least illegal. For business to monopolize and thus dictate prices is illegal. The use of duress to evoke a contract promise is illegal. To rob another is a crime.

Jim imagined two ways to get his children, the first legal and essentially persuasion, to purchase them, and the second illegal and essentially force, to steal them. On the raft with Huck, Jim might have used force to prevent being handed over to the slave hunters; but once Huck was in the canoe and out of physical reach, Jim's only power base was persuasion.

There are complexities about power not reflected in Figure 3-5. One might ask, "What is the power base of the individual exercising his right to vote?" and "Why do legislators depend most heavily on persuasion to get their jobs done?" In our federal and state legal system, we have allocated authority and procedures among four, not three, units. To achieve polyarchy, nonleaders have reserved some of the authority power base to themselves by the vote. This reservation is designed to require that leaders compete for the support of nonleaders. Therein nonleaders control leaders. Furthermore, in the act of competing, leaders are theoretically limited to the persuasion power base, although they often rely on influence developed through patronage and support of special interests. A legislature, because it has many members, must function on the basis of internal persuasion, bargaining, and compromise. To the extent that the chief executive is dependent upon acts of the legislature he must rely on persuasion and influence. He must compete for support with legislative leaders. The supreme courts have little power to impose their decisions on executives, legislators, and the people. Therefore, the chief expression of their decisions is in the form of opinions containing elaborate efforts at demonstrating to, and thus persuading, others of the rectitude and efficacy of their decisions.

THE SOCIAL ENGINEER

Power

If one can accept the proposition that legal systems are likely to exist in all groups, state and nonstate, then he can fully evaluate the power positions he possesses as well as the power positions of those with whom he is in conflict. He may see that in some groups he is a part of recognized officialdom and occupies power bases of authority and influence. In others, he has persuasion. In still others, he may be horrified to find that he controls through force. In any case, his task as a social engineer may be easy or difficult depending on the relevant group and his power base. Attention to his power bases and relevant groups will help him recognize the organized clusters of activities that constitute his roles in recurrent and regularized activity and to identify the social controls to which he is subject in each role as arising out of the behavioral foundations of social structure. The sources of his sense of injustice and other strains can be more rationally calculated and controlled.

Behavior

The basic activity of a social engineer has five facets: (1) problem observation, or perception, (2) problem description, or definition, (3) solution development, (4) persuasion or other forms of resistance to challenge, and (5) compromise. These are more specific than the functions generally attributed to behavioral scientists—that is, study for understanding, prediction, and control. In any realistic efforts at social problem solving, competitive notions of what ought to be exist. To the behavioral scientist "control" is only manipulation. At least two elements in addition to the behavioral scientist are included in the personality of a social engineer: the philosopher and the politician. The philosopher acts with or as the behavioral scientist in problem perception. He must empirically study the sources of his strain until he understands the nature of his or his group's problem. Then he must be able to communicate an awareness of the existence of the problem and its nature by adequate description. Now when he acts to control by developing a solution to the problem calling for some change in recurrent and regularized activity between two or more people, he is in the realm of the "ought," the realm of values; and the behavioral scientist is left behind.

Actual control requires exercises of authority or persuasion. Many in positions of authority perform enormous parts of their duties by acts of persuasion. The legislature with the duty to participate in the enactment of statutes engages in and is subject to much persuasion and influence. Persuasion is a political art. It is necessary because others will challenge one's perception of the existence of a problem, his understanding of the problem, his definition of the problem, and his solution for the problem. Seldom does one fully persuade others on any issue. More often there is some degree of successful challenge. But if the challenge itself is an act of persuasion in some degree successfully challenged, compromise is necessary because effective social problem solving often requires the cooperation of those with the divergent urges. The compromise may be to submit the divergent solutions as claims to the legal system of the group for settlement. The settlement may involve making choices (by courts) among such claims, or it may involve employing bargaining machinery (by legislature) of the legal system. The machinery for making choices may also rely on bargaining techniques. By whatever decision process, if clear choice is not possible, bargaining is the essential activity necessary to compromise.

Bargaining[5]

Bargaining is possible in most groups because social indoctrination about norms and views of reality produce individuals and groups with about the same values. Further, many social groups are made up of the same individuals who stimulate bargaining between groups. There is basic agreement among most about the common sharing of primary and instrumental goals and the need for associated action to eliminate obstacles to those goals. Pluralism, interdependence, and disagreement make bargaining necessary, possible, and profitable. And bargaining is the behavioral connecting link between persuasion and compromise. The political activity of persuasion, bargaining, and compromise engaged in by most people in most roles in most groups is necessary activity.

JURISPRUDENCE[6]

For a moment, tying together thoughts about justice, law, and social engineering, it is not unreasonable to conclude that all are necessary to associated activity. This necessity may be demonstrated by showing their relationship in science, philosophy, and art. Science can develop understandings of behavior. Specifically, scientific jurisprudence as a behavioral science can develop understandings, make predictions, and control variable of behavior that eliminate or create obstacles to the attainment of desires—the behavior of justice. Philosophy can aid in developing understandings of justice and generate solutions for removing obstacles to goals on the basis of value judgments of what ought to be. When it does so, it is philosophical jurisprudence. Art involves creative activity. In the art of jurisprudence, creative activity involves employing claims, persuasion, bargaining, and compromise. Thereby, the law tool evokes changes in norms, values and sanctions inducing changes in recurrent and regularized interactions among people so that justice may be more nearly realized.

The individual may occupy differing power bases in the various groups to which he belongs. These differing bases affect only the quality of opportunity for practicing the science, philosophy, and art of jurisprudence. They do not affect the existence of opportunity itself. The nature of the group—large, small, state, nonstate, and so forth—also affects only the quality of opportunity, not the existence of opportunity to participate in social problem solving. According to such a view, social engineering and jurisprudence are for everybody and not just for a few thousand specialists. The understanding generated by empirical observation of the behavioral scientist has its equivalents in many groups as the understanding generated by some of its members. That is why for many people sociology can be defined as the science of the obvious. Cumulative effort at devising means for relief from the commonly felt strain arising out of a problem often results in claims, persuasion, bargaining, and compromise about the existence or nature of the problem and the optimum solution. Jurisprudence is truly the background of all associated activity.

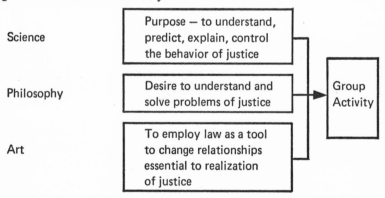

Figure 3 - 6 JURISPRUDENCE

Some very specific research needs to be done to support or refute the assumptions of this model. A systematic study of a variety of nonstate groups to determine the prevalence of the existence of legal systems, social engineering activity, and jurisprudence still needs to be done. Llewellyn and Hoebel started and called for more. There have been some tentative responses to the challenge.[7]

NOTES

1. Preconditions and conditions of a legal system are drawn from Karl Llewellyn, "The Normative, the Legal, and the Law Jobs: The Problem of Juristic Method," *Yale Law Journal,* 49:8 (June 1940), 1355-1400. See also Karl Llewellyn and Adamson Hoebel, *The Cheyenne Way* (Norman, Okla.: University of Oklahoma Press, 1941).

2. Robert A. Dahl and Charles E. Lindblom, *Politics, Economics and Welfare* (New York: Harper & Row Torch Book, 1963), pp. 99-109.

3. Variations of power and its subsets abound. The one developed in this work is an elaboration of a Llewellyn construct *(supra)* and a Weber construct [Max Rheinstein, ed., *Max Weber on Law in Economy and Society,* trans. Max Rheinstein and Edward Shils (Cambridge, Mass.: Harvard University Press, 1954)]. Weber, by the way, did not hesitate to refer to authority systems as legal systems and legal systems as authority power bases. Other variations can be found in Harold D. Lasswell and Abraham Kaplan, *Power and Society* (New Haven, Conn.: Yale University Press, 1950), and in Peter Bachrach and Morton S. Baratz, *Power and Poverty* (London: Oxford University Press, 1970). Management literature is preoccupied with the subject.

4. Hohfeld set up a pairing of jural opposites and jural correlatives as follows:

Jural opposites	right	privilege	power	immunity
	no-right	duty	disability	liability

Jural correlatives	right	privilege	power	immunity
	duty	no-right	liability	disability

The pairings were intended, among other things, to demonstrate legal meanings of the words. The concept "power" as he employed it referred to one's "control over a given legal relation as against another" and is far more limited than the meaning of the word as used in this work. This set of jural opposites and correlatives is very useful, however, in ascertaining the nature of specific examples of power as authority inuring to individual benefit or detriment. See Wesley N. Hohfeld, *Fundamental Legal Conceptions,* ed. Walter W. Cook (New Haven, Conn.: Yale University Press, 1946), pp. 3-9, for the chart and the quotation.

5. Dahl and Lindblom, *op. cit.,* pp. 324-365. This is a summary of the subject of bargaining as explained by Dahl and Lindblom.

6. The discussion of jurisprudence as science, philosophy, and art of justice and jurisprudence as necessary to all associated activity is based on the "Prologue: On Jurisprudence" in John C.H. Wu, *Cases and Materials on Jurisprudence* (St. Paul, Minn.: West Publishing Co., 1958), pp. 5-14.

7. H. R. Hartzler and Harry Allan, *Introduction to Law: A Functional Approach* (Glenview, Ill.: Scott, Foresman, 1969), pp. 64–69, and "Legal Theories of Roscoe Pound and Karl Llewellyn: Their Application to the Study of Behavior Within Business Organization," 5, *American Business Law Journal,* 1 (1967).

4

CONFLICT AND GOAL ACHIEVEMENT

Most people in most groups hold power bases of persuasion, and where law is the element of social control affecting their lives, they tend not to break the law. Unfortunately, many tend to fantasize about it and thus take no rational active part in employing the law to affect the quality of their lives. Those occupying this power base who do not break the law or fantasize about it as a recourse to relieve the strains of social conditions including social control either work to preserve the legal foundations of existing social structure or they work to change it.[1] If one perceives the existing order as imperfectly removing obstacles to attainment of his desires or perceives it as an obstacle in some respect, he tends to persuade others of the need for change in the law. If he perceives the trend of changes in a legal system as posing obstacles to desires already adequately satisfied, he attempts to persuade others of the need for retention of the existing law. The social engineering then taking place is in an arena of conflict between ideas about the nature of and need for stability and security and the nature of and need for progress. In that arena, the divergent urges underlying the conflict may assume the proportions of competing claims for recognition and protection by the legal system of the group.

AUTHORITATIVE GENERALIZATIONS

Roscoe Pound has observed an interesting process in the history of claims-conflict resolution.[2] A legal system usually affords, fully or in part, a remedy for one of the competing claims. In some degree, a claim, demand or expectation is recognized and protected by law if the legal system makes any decision or even if it refuses to decide. To the extent that individuals and groups persist over time in presenting similar claims for settlement before a legal system and to the extent that similar remedies are devised, authoritative generalizations can be articulated about the remedies. For example, when the remedy has been to recognize a claim that one ought to be able to control and use what he has or acquires against a claim that objects ought to be available for use by anybody who desires them regardless of who is claiming control or use, a generalization about private property can be made. The system is giving remedies protecting private property. The authoritative generalization can be expressed as a rule: Whoever knowingly takes the property of another with intent permanently to deprive him thereof shall surrender the property to the owner and be punished for the wrongful appropriation. The authoritative generalization can range from a very broad one to a very specific one. The more specific are called rules of law.

RIGHT-DUTY RELATIONSHIPS[3]

A rule of law contains within it a more or less explicit statement about the relationship enforced by the legal system upon members of the group. It does so by expressing the correlative rights and duties of persons whose behavior is to be channeled. The rule expressed above in effect confers upon one party a right to control and use what he has and acquires and upon another the duty not to interfere with that control and use. Such right-duty correlatives are an important part of a legal system's ability to regularize recurrent interactions among persons. The conflict underlying competing claims has been utilized by the legal system to contribute to the nature of social structure and social control.

Not everyone is satisfied with the right-duty relationships generated out of the claims-remedies-generalizations-rules process. To the extent that the system produces results that fall short of desires and evoke feelings of injustice because of the limited supremacy of the processes of persuasion, bargaining, and compromise, strains remain or newly arise. Reaction sets in, and old claims are changed to some degree, or new claims are submitted to the legal system for recognition and protection. The social engineers, aspiring to rationality in problem solving and the achievement of other instrumental and primary goals, are then at work. The process is continuance. (See Figure 4-1.)

Figure 4-1 represents the eternal conflict between those who seek progress and those who seek security. The effort of one to eliminate perceived obstacles to the attainment of his goals threatens to create obstacles to goals already satisfactorily achieved by the other. In the mid-nineteenth century, business had a very favorable legal environment. It benefited by virtual immunity from liability to consumers harmed in life and limb by defective products.[4] Consumers persisted in claiming greater protection from defective products. Business's response was to resist the claim and stand on its legal protections provided by privity of contract theory, which held that no one could recover damages from a manufacturer unless he had purchased the harm-causing defective product directly from him. Consumer rights only arose out of contract duties voluntarily assumed by manufacturers. If the consumer bought from a middleman, he was not in privity of contract with the manufacturer. Few consumers bought directly from manufacturers.

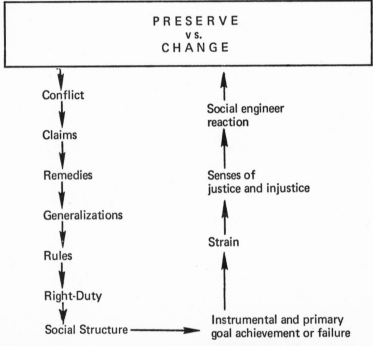

Figure 4 – 1   CONFLICT AND SOCIAL CHANGE BY LAW

The battle was fought on basic grounds of survival. Who was to have the benefit of a favorable legal climate conducive to survival? Consumers claimed that defective products were maiming and killing them. Manufacturers claimed that to impose liability for such harm on them would be to drive them out of business.

Gradually, because of constant effort of consumers to acquire greater legal protection, more remedies were granted to consumers. They acquired greater rights against manufacturers, who were burdened with greater duties. New rules developed in this sequence: (1) Regardless of an absence of privity, manufacturers owed a duty of care to consumers in the making of inherently dangerous products such as guns and poison; (2) the duty was extended to other products such as automobiles; (3) manufacturers' affirmations of fact about the condition of food products became express warranty obligations, even in the absence of privity; (4) consumer rights developed to the point where manufacturers' affirmations of fact about any kind of product had to be true; (5) duties called "implied warranties" to provide fit, fair quality food products were imposed in the absence of privity and even in the absence of express warranty; (6) the same implied warranties created consumer rights with respect to products other than food; (7) during this development manufacturers tried to avoid these liabilities by inducing consumers to agree to manufacturer disclaimers of liability in the retail sales contracts (the disclaimer was disguised as a warranty); and (8) the disclaimer was held to be illegal. The social engineering on behalf of consumers has gone so far that some courts have discussed the possibility of making manufacturers absolutely liable for all injuries caused by defective products a consumer could not protect against. This process of evolving claims-conflict has taken 100 years.[5]

In conclusion, Figure 4-1 demonstrates how conflict may be converted into goal-achieving social structure by a legal system in a dynamic society. Refer again to Pound's statement about law and social engineering on page 33.

JURAL POSTULATES[6]

Pound further attempted to generalize about the common nature of claims over long periods of time. He saw the constantly changing claims-conflicts falling into five very broad categories. It seemed to him that in a civilized society a man ought to be able to assume that others would not commit intentional aggressions against him; that one ought to be able to control and use what he has or acquires; that others will act in good faith by making promises reasonably expected of them, by performing those promises as made, and by restoring to one what is his but which has fallen into another's hands by mistake or other events; that others will exercise due care not to create unreasonable risks for him; and that others will restrain their holdings and keep them within proper bounds so that he is not harmed. These categories of claims he called "jural postulates" because they could be regarded as the five most fundamental assumptions in the legal system of any civilized society.

SOCIAL INTERESTS[7]

In any specific claims-conflict, the choice made as to the claims, or parts of claims, to be recognized and protected in the legal system by the granting of a remedy may be controlled by social utility considerations affected by perceptions of the social interest. That is, the recognition of specific claims, demands, and expectations based on jural postulates of individuals can resul from the legal system's sensitivity to social interests. Then the legal system can serve coalescent individual and social needs. Pound claimed the existenc of six such social interests: (1) social interest in general security of the group as a viable whole; (2) social interest in the security of social institutions, which are constituted out of selective, regularized, and regulated interactions by various social controls such as values, which are beliefs that legitimize, norms, which are standards that regulate, and sanctions; (3) therefrom promotion of general morals as a social interest naturally follows; (4) promotion of the conservation of social resources; (5) promotion of progress; and (6) promotion of individual life according to standards considered deserving of humanity.

JURAL POSTULATES AND PRIMARY GOALS

Recognition and protection of jural postulate claims promote these social interests, and promotion of the social interests promotes individual interests. But jural postulates are assumptions about relationships relevant to legal systems. As such, they are not the most fundamental of individual interests. Primary goals are of most fundamental interest to individuals. Ho are primary and instrumental goals related to Pound's jural postulates and social interests? The motive to postulate jurally must be by using a legal system to cause the elimination of common obstacles in ordinary social life to attainment of desires. Aggressions, interference with use and enjoyment of property, absences of good faith, creation of unreasonable risks, and failure to restrain holdings within proper bounds—all stand as common behavior blocking primary goal achievement of others.

An example of the last postulate involves the neighborhood dog: If he is not kept at home but is instead allowed to roam, killing evergreen shrubb at will, at the least an esthetic satisfaction primary goal is blocked.

SOCIAL INTERESTS AND INSTRUMENTAL GOALS

In handling specific claims-conflicts, legal system recognition and support of the jural postulates by decision techniques appropriate to goals and social interests involved would be a rational system. Resulting elimination of obstacles to the attainment of desires would evoke a sense of freedom. The best political environment for appropriate decision techniques in a rational legal system would require fundamentally equal power and control over officials by nonleaders—that is, some form of democracy (polyarchy) conducive to a subjective sense of equality in each individual. Effective protection of existing institutions, resources, and relationships by the legal system would evoke a satisfying sense of stability and security, while inducing results compatible with felt needs of change for better goal achievement would evoke a satisfying sense of progress. Furthermore, if he is also rational, one perceiving that others are jurally postulating the same assumptions as his and having their claims, demands, and expectations recognized and protected by law, may have a sense of appropriate inclusion. This utopian functioning of a legal system would undoubtedly result in a perfect sense of justice by all members of the group.

POSTULATES, INTERESTS, AND GOALS

Of course, given social complexity and the variety and intensity of divergence of urges which inevitably arises therefrom, such perfect justice is probably never possible. However, one could see in a system aspiring to such goals increasing satisfaction of want and elimination of waste and friction in human life and ever more appropriate combinations of stability and progress toward attainment of the social goals of promoting general security of social institutions, general morals, conservation of social resources, general progress, and high quality of individual life. Particularly as other social interests tend to promote the quality of life for individuals in the system, the individuals will tend to experience increasing attainment of their primary goals: to survive, to experience physiological gratification, love and affection, respect, self-respect, power and control, skill, enlightenment, prestige esthetics satisfactions, and so on.

Figure 4-2 relates primary and instrumental goals to jural postulates and social interests, all dependent on a core of justice. It demonstrates that primary goals give rise to jural postulates in a legal system. Together, primary goals and jural postulates in a given society fashion the specific forms that the instrumental goals will have as the legal system acts to promote social interests. Independently and together, the parts of the four concepts will fashion the sense of justice, injustice, or mix of the two that an individual will experience in his interactions with others, with the group, and with the legal system.

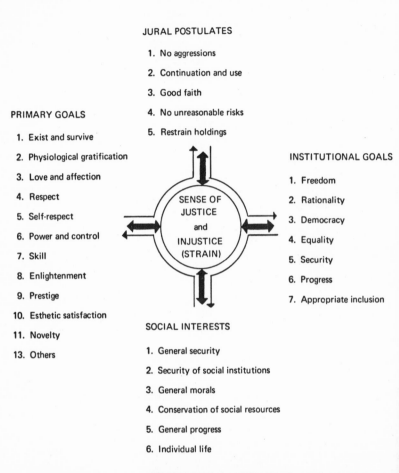

JURAL POSTULATES

1. No aggressions
2. Continuation and use
3. Good faith
4. No unreasonable risks
5. Restrain holdings

PRIMARY GOALS

1. Exist and survive
2. Physiological gratification
3. Love and affection
4. Respect
5. Self-respect
6. Power and control
7. Skill
8. Enlightenment
9. Prestige
10. Esthetic satisfaction
11. Novelty
13. Others

SENSE OF JUSTICE and INJUSTICE (STRAIN)

INSTITUTIONAL GOALS

1. Freedom
2. Rationality
3. Democracy
4. Equality
5. Security
6. Progress
7. Appropriate inclusion

SOCIAL INTERESTS

1. General security
2. Security of social institutions
3. General morals
4. Conservation of social resources
5. General progress
6. Individual life

Figure 4 – 2   POSTULATES, INTERESTS AND GOALS

Suggestions for further research: This model makes assumptions about cause and effect relationships, which should be tested under controlled research conditions. What are the probabilities that those in a group who are in conflict about primary goal achievement will make a claim before the group's legal system that can be classified according to a jural postulate? Specifically, how, if at all, do the jural postulates as claims shape political and social institutions for instrumental goal achievement? Does it follow that in approaching achievement of instrumental goals one will perceive social utility that can be classified according to social interests? Does one tend to perceive primary goal achievement in enhancement of social interests by a legal system? What is the net sense of justice or injustice (strain) that results from these interactions? Perhaps research about these questions can provide a basis for some quantifications about justice or injustice within a group.

NOTES

1. These four forms of reaction to strain (break the law, fantasize, work to preserve, work to change) arising from operations of a legal system are adapted from Smelser's discussion of attitudinal and behavioral reaction to strain. Neil Smelser, *The Sociology of Economic Life,* Englewood Cliffs, N.J.: Prentice-Hall (1963).

2. Roscoe Pound, *The Spirit of the Common Law* (Boston: Beacon Press, 1963). Much of the following discussion is based on Pound's work.

3. Hohfeld's pairings of jural opposites and correlatives set out in note 4, Chapter 3, provide more specific descriptive word tools to express rights, duties, and the absence of rights and duties. Here, "right" and "duty" are used as substitutes for most of those specifics: privilege, power, immunity, no-right, disability, and liability.

4. Winterbottom v. Wright, L.R. 3 H.H. 330, 1868, 152 E.R. 402.

5. The new rules sequence is represented by the following cases: (1) Thomas v. Winchester, 6 N.Y. 397 (1852); (2) McPherson v. Buick Motor Co., 217 N.Y. 382, 111 N.E. 1050 (1916); (3) Lane v. C.S. Swanson and Sons, 278 P 2nd 723 (1955); (4) Worley v. Procter and Gamble Manufacturing Co., 253 S.W. 2d 532 (1952); (5) Jacob E. Decker & Sons, Inc. v. Capps, 139 Tex. 609, 164 S.W. 2d 828 (1942); (6) Henningsen *et al.* v. Bloomfield Motors *et al.,* 32 N.Y. 358, 161 A2d 69 (1960); (7) Shafer v. Reo Motors, Inc., 108 F Supp. 659 (1952) and 205 F 2d 685 (1953), Payne v. Valley Motor Sales, Inc., 124 SE 2d 622 (1961); (8) Henningsen, *supra.* Absolute liability theory: Rylands and Harrocks v. Fletcher, House of Lords, L.R. 3 H.L. 330 (1068), Escola v. Coca Cola Bottling Co. of Fresno, 24 Cal. 2d 453, 150 P. 2d 436 (1944).

6. Pound, op. cit.

7. *Ibid.,* pp. 208–210.

5

LAW – GOVERNMENT

The next problem of importance in determining the relationship of justice, legal systems, and social structure is to get more deeply into the specialized system of a group wherein the process of optimizing conflict as a base for building social structure takes place—a legal system and government.[1] The two are inseparable. Fundamentally, government exists when the behavior of governing takes place. Most simply stated, government is the behavior of control of man by man wherein at the extreme the system would be one of men and not of laws. Law exists when the behavior of control of men by rules exits, wherein the system at the extreme would be one of laws and not of men.

Pure government and pure law are mutually exclusive. Under pure government, an absolute tyrant would be able to control all other men by the exercise of unconstrained whim in no discernible pattern. Those subject to control could never informally create constraints on the tyrant by adjusting their behavior in advance to his regularized patterns of behavior, which could be generalized as authoritative and perceived as rules. There would be no standards for judgment. For pure law to exist, there would be a rule in the form of a ceremonial formula for every human eventuality. Al behavior would be controlled by rules as ritual ceremony to the exclusion of exercises of discretion or judgment by a leader. A leader could never govern under such a system.

Either extreme is probably impossible in the law-government system of any group. Thus any group, when the necessary preconditions exist, will have a mix of law and government elements. Some system mixes will have the law element dominant, as in most democracies; and some will have the government element dominant, as in most dictatorships. In addition, in any system there will be variations. In some subareas of human authority subject to the law-government system, the law element will dominate and in others the government element will dominate whether or not the total system is characterized as one of men or one of laws. Furthermore, in some subareas at one time the law element may dominate the mix and at another the government element may dominate. Any system can be visualized as occupying a place somewhere on a continuum between a law pole and a government pole. (See Figure 5-1.)

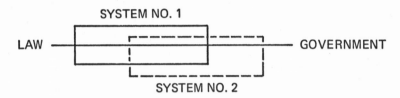

Figure 5 – 1   LAW-GOVERNMENT

DECISION PROCESSES[2]

Formal Irrational

In either of these systems, there are four possible kinds of relationship between the discretion of those performing the function of governing and the rules and ceremonies of the system controlling that discretion. Max Weber has identified these relationships as part of the law-finding or law-making process and the law-application process. The formal irrational process and relationship severely limits the use of discretion in decision making by a judge or administrator. Formality *is* the decision process. For example, law requiring a draft by lottery eliminates human discretion in choosing who shall be drafted from among those subject to the draft. To say that such decision making is formal irrational is not to say that the process is bad—or good—but only that human reason and judgment play no part. Obedience by recognized officials to the formality of the law makes the decision. In the formality, there is no standard with which judgment can work. Trial by battle and trial by ordeal are examples from the past.

Formal Rational

The formal rational process and relationship permits more human discretion and judgment, but discretion is constrained by the logical requirements of the rule—that is, the form of the rule. A syllogism is employed in the decision process. A major premise for the syllogism would be a rule such as, The taking of the life of another with malice aforethought is first degree murder. The minor premise would be fabricated out of the facts of a particular case. John took the life of another with malice aforethought. Judgment may have been exercised in selecting the major premise and determining the substance of the minor premise; but after that the conclusion is inevitable: John committed first-degree murder.

Substantive Rational

Substantive rational decision making shifts the emphasis from the controlling nature of rules to rules as servants of desired ends. One might call the product of the formal rational process "justice," but the substantive rational process begins with feelings about justice as a primary input Given the fact of a conflict, what decision does a sense of justice dictate? Perceptions of justice and facts control the nature of the decision, the remedy, and any rule or other authoritative generalization to be drawn. Prior to a given case, it may have been the law that one not in privity of contract with a manufacturer could not recover from the manufacturer on implied warranty theory for personal injuries received because of the unmerchantability of the product. However, if officials making the decision feel strongly enough that justice requires a recovery against the manufacturer, under the circumstances they may grant a remedy accordingly and create the basis in precedent for a change in the law. Here the law–government system has had less affect in restraining the discretion of officials. Judges are constrained to the extent that such decisions customarily must be rationalized in their legal opinions as serving social policy, or by trends in precedent and analogy or by reinterpretation of previously mistaken meanings or purposes of rules

Substantive Irrational

Finally, nearer the government pole, a law–government system may tolerate some substantive irrational official behavior. The behavior is irrational, not in the sense that it is illogical, but in that it is not necessarily related to the goals of the group. Instead it is evoked by the whim of the official rather than according to accepted standards. A young man is threatened by a policeman because he has long hair. A bureaucrat rejects a claim because of the race of the claimant. A judge acquits a defendant in order to avoid possible review and reversal of his decision. Here, operationally at least, rules seem to have little constraining effect on the exercise of discretion, and the behavior may not be consistent enough to provide a basis for making authoritative generalizations to guide future decision making or behavior.

In one case, an eighteen-year-old black man was drafted contrary to the requirements that one be nineteen. Unfortunately, a rumor in his home town scandalized the community. He was thought to be in love with a white girl. The girl's father was a member of the draft board. By the time he was nineteen, he had been drafted, fought in Vietnam, been severely wounded, been discharged and become a student at the University of Massachusetts with G.I. Bill benefits.

In rational authority systems, arbitrariness has no place. It amounts to behavior based on one's will alone and not upon any course of reasoning and exercise of judgment. To behave in an arbitrary[3] manner is to act capriciously without accepted determining principle. One who is arbitrary is behaving as though he is absolute in power. It is extreme tyrannical and despotic behavior. A tyrant acts without fair or substantial cause derived from the law of the authority system. The difference between a free and an arbitrary government is that in the former limits are assigned to administrators and others by allocations of authority and procedure, but the latter results from the will of administrators or officials. Authority and procedures are allocated to recognized officials in most systems to enable them to function for the benefit of the group, to protect individual rights, and to limit their wills to act for their own benefit or according to their own prejudices. In the latter instances they are said to act capriciously, though some personal or inappropriate system of values explicitly or implicitly excluded is probably the basis of a prejudiced act.

Figure 5-2 represents the place of prejudice, arbitrariness, and capriciousness in an authority system on a continuum. The law pole represents a system in which all human discretion is eliminated. Outcomes are determined by rigid law ceremonies, often without relevance to the problem.

The government pole represents a system in which there are no determining principles and one man exercises the power of life and death over all others in a completely unpredictable manner.

Formal irrational (F/I) decision making is near the law pole. A flip of a coin determines a course of action—what grade to give, who gets tenure. It is irrational in that once the method of decision is chosen, the reason of man no longer is necessary in arriving at an outcome.

Formal rational (F/R) decision making proceeds from rules. One who makes 96 earns an "A." The student made a 96. He earns an "A." One who writes a book, publishes three articles, and serves on five committees earns tenure. A faculty member has written a book, published three articles, and served on five committees. He earns tenure. The formality of the decision process is the syllogism. The reason of the decision maker is directed by the syllogism to the ultimate conclusion.

LAW MAKING AND APPLICATION

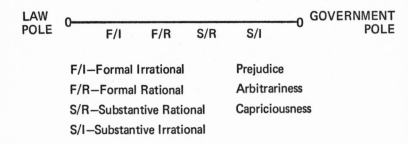

Figure 5 – 2

Substantive rational (S/R) decision making proceeds on a foundation of standards. A student's grade depends on the professor's judgment of the level of knowledge, skills, and attitudes attained by the student. The superior student gets the "A." The reasoning power of the decision maker is guided by the policy standard and is exercised in judging the quality of student behavior. Similarly, faculty tenure depends on the decision maker's judgment of the quality of performance according to stated substantive standards such as excellence in two and adequacy in one of the areas of teaching, research, and service.

If the decision maker flunks a student who made a 96 or whose level of knowledge, skills, and attitudes would be judged superior by reasonable men, or if he denies tenure to one who by reasonable men would be judged to be excellent in two fields and adequate in the other, then the decision maker has employed an inappropriate decision technique. He has either acted F/I (he flipped a coin) or his behavior has been substantive irrational (S/I).

Substantive irrational decision making is based on prejudice, caprice, or arbitrariness, contrary to rules or standards of authority and procedures allocated to administrators and others to act for the benefit of the whole group and to limit their wills to act for their own benefit or according to their own prejudices—that is, inappropriate rules, standards, and values.

In most law-government systems only formal rationality and substantive rationality are commonly acceptable methods of decision making. If the decision maker working under rules arrives at a decision not possible according to the syllogism, he has exceeded the bounds of his authority and his right to decide. If the decision maker, subject to accepted policy standards, arrives at a decision which no reasonable man using the same standards could agree with, then the decision maker has abused his discretion. He has exceeded his authority and right to decide. The motive of the decision maker is not important. For example, he may claim that he has acted for the good of the university. But the rules and standards have been developed with that end in mind, and to depart from the rules for whatever noble purpose is capricious, arbitrary, and/or prejudiced. The proper behavior is to change the rules if they are incompatible with the good of the university. Civil disobedience by officials is dangerous.

Finally, one who makes an effort to change the rules and standards must do so only on the basis of due regard for the rights of those who have relied on the old ones. A student told for most of a semester that 96 is an "A" and then on the last day of class that 99 is an "A" is just as much a victim of caprice, arbitrariness, and/or prejudice as one who with a 96 is denied an "A" without a change in the rule. Similarly, a faculty person told for six years that an award of tenure depends on a certain level of performance and in his tenure year that the performance level has been changed is just as much a victim of caprice, arbitrariness, and/or prejudice as one who with the performance level achieved is denied tenure without a change in standards.

The following is a good example of substantive irrational law making and application:

Heads or Tails

De balena vero sufficit, si rex habeat caput, et regina caudam.
Bracton, 1.3, c. 3.

Latin from the books of the Laws of England, which taken along with the context, means, that of all whales captured by anybody on the coast of that land, the King as Honorary Grand Harpooneer, must have the head, and the Queen be respectfully presented with the tail—a division which, in the whale, is much like having an apple; there is no intermediate remainder. Now as this law, under a modified form, is to this day in force in England; and as it offers in various respects a strange anomaly touching the general law of Fast-and Loose-Fish, it is here treated of in a separate chapter, on the same courteous principle that prompts the English railways to be at the expense of a separate car, specially reserved for the accommodation of royalty. In the first place, in curious proof of the fact that the above-mentioned law is still in force, I proceed to lay before you a circumstance that happened within the last two years.

It seems that some honest mariners of Dover, or Sandwich, or some one of the Cinque Ports, had after a hard chase succeeded in killing and beaching a fine whale which they had originally descried afar off from the shore. Now the Cinque Ports are partially or somehow under the jurisdiction of a sort of policeman or beadle, called a Lord Warden. Holding the office directly from the crown, I believe, all the royal emoluments incident to the Cinque Port territories become by assignment his. By some writers this office is called a *sinecure*. But not so. Because the Lord Warden is busily employed at times in fobbing his perquisites; which are his chiefly by virtue of that same fobbing of them.

Now when these poor sunburnt mariners bare-footed and with their trousers rolled high up on their eely legs, had wearily hauled their fat fish high and dry, promising themselves a good £150 from the precious oil and bone; and in fantasy sipping rare tea with their wives, and good ale with their cronies, upon the strength of their respective shares; up steps a very learned and most Christian and charitable gentleman, with a copy of Blackstone under his arm; and laying it upon the whale's head, he says—"Hands off! This fish, my masters, is a Fast-Fish. I seize it as the Lord Warden's."

Upon this the poor mariners in their respectful consternation—so truly English—knowing not what to say, fall to vigorously scratching their heads all round; meanwhile ruefully glancing from the whale to the stranger. But that did in nowise mend the matter, or at all soften the hard heart of the learned gentleman with the copy of Blackstone. At length one of them, after long scratching about for his ideas, made bold to speak.

"Please sir, who is the Lord Warden?"

"The Duke."

"But the Duke had nothing to do with taking this fish."

"It is his."

"We have been at great trouble, and peril, and some expense, and is all that to go to the Duke's benefit; we getting nothing at all for our pains but our blisters?"

"It is his."

"Is the Duke so very poor as to be forced to this desperate mode of getting a livelihood?"

"It is his."

"I thought to relieve my old bedridden mother by part of my share of this whale."

"It is his."

"Won't the Duke be content with a quarter or a half?"

"It is his."

In a word, the whale was seized and sold, and his Grace the Duke of Wellington received the money. Thinking that viewed in some particular lights, the case might by a bare possibility in some small degree be deemed, under the circumstances, a rather hard one, an honest clergyman of the town respectfully addressed a note to his Grace, begging him to take the case of those unfortunate mariners into full consideration. To which my Lord Duke in substance replied (both letters were published) that he had already done so, and received the money, and would be obliged to the reverend gentleman if for the future he (the reverend gentleman) would decline meddling with other people's business. Is this the still militant old man, standing at the corners of the three kingdoms, on all hands coercing alms of beggars?

It will readily be seen that in this case the alleged right of the Duke to the whale was a delegated one from the Sovereign. We must needs inquire then on what principle the Sovereign is originally invested with that right. The law itself has already been set forth. But Plowden gives us reason for it. Says Plowden, the whale so caught belongs to the King and Queen, "because of its superior excellence." And by the soundest commentators this has ever been held a cogent argument in such matters.

But why should the King have the head, the Queen the tail? A reason for that, ye lawyers?

In his treaties on "Queen-Gold," or Queen pinmoney, an old King's Bench author, one William Prynne, thus discourseth: "Ye tail is ye Queen's, that ye Queen's wardrobe may be supplied with ye whalebone." Now this was written at a time when the black limber bone of the Greenland or Right Whale was largely used in ladies' bodices. But this same bone is not in the tail; it is in the head, which is a sad mistake for a sagacious lawyer like Prynne. But is the Queen a mermaid, to be presented with a tail? An allegorical meaning may lurk here.

There are two royal fish so styled by the English law writers—the whale and the sturgeon; both royal property under certain limitations, and nominally supplying the tenth branch of the crown's ordinary revenue. I know not that any other author has hinted of the matter; but by inference it seems to me that the sturgeon must be divided in the same way as the whale, the King receiving the highly dense and elastic head peculiar to that fish, which symbolically regarded, may possibly be humorously grounded upon some presumed congeniality. And thus there seems a reason in all things, even in law.[4]

Social Dynamics

Most behavior by officials in a law–government system falls in a range from the formal rational to the substantive rational. Many reasons for this fact are to be found in social structure generally and in law–government structures specifically. These will be dealt with later. Now, however, it should be recalled that officials of law–government systems, being human, are likely to react to changes or absence of changes in those systems much as anyone else might. They are usually not deviants. If the system, as perceived, is blocking instrumental and primary goal achievement in the group, the official is likely to seek changes to bring the system into operational compatibility with his sense of justice. As opportunities present themselves, he is likely to function on a substantive rational basis. But if proposed changes in the system are perceived as creating new blocks to goal achievement and as impairing acceptable past social structure in the process, the official is likely to act to preserve existing "law and order." In such circumstances, the official is acting in a formal rational manner. Either way the official is probably trying to relieve some strain the working of the system is creating for him. Probably few officials become dropouts by electing one of the other two alternatives for relieving strain—criminal activity or fantasy. Or at least no more engage in this activity than the proportionate share of the population at large. Some research should be done on the subject.

Good examples of both types of common official behavior can be found in the Johnson v. Cadillac[5] and MacPherson v. Buick[6] cases, which played a part in the common law evolution of consumer protection summarized earlier. These cases proceeded through the courts at the same time, the Johnson case in the federal courts and the MacPherson case in the New York state courts. The majority in the Johnson case held to the established law and applied it in a formal rational manner. Concern was expressed for proposed changes which would enlarge manufacturer product liability. A dissenting judge avowed that life and limb of human beings were at stake and insisted that old law requiring a privity relationship as a prerequisite to liability of manufacturers give way to greater need for consumer protection. The majority in the MacPherson case, speaking through Benjamin Cardozo, deduced that law suitable for the days of the horse and buggy was not suitable to the automobile age. Judge Willard Bartlett dissented on the basis that the majority had changed the law (i.e., there is no duty of care owed to a consumer in the absence of privity of contract except where the product is inherently dangerous) to a new one (i.e., that manufacturers owe a duty of care not to supply negligently caused defective products harmful to consumers). Bartlett would have decided the case using the old law in a formal rational manner as did the majority in the Johnson case. Cardozo decided the case relying heavily on substantive considerations about changing technology, values, and interests, as would the dissenting judge in the Johnson case. As it turned out, the MacPherson case decision dominated the evolutionary course of consumer protection as the Johnson case law became a thing of the past. It is interesting to note finally that the MacPherson rule, since its acceptance, has been applied in a formal rational manner.

OPERATIONAL PREDICTABILITY

There is usually enough complexity and uncertainty about specific social interests mixed with variations in ability and sensibility of officials that the two cannot operate in lock step in all cases. With officials making decisions some on a formal rational basis and some on a substantive rational basis in similar cases, and some on formal rational bases and substantive rational bases with dissimilar cases, the predictability of outcome of cases becomes uncertain. Also, in cases where the law–government system's formal rational process is dominant, decisions are more predictable than in cases where a substantive rational process is about to dominate. At the extremes, the operational predictability of the system can be illustrated as in Figure 5-3.

0————————————————————————————————————0
  Predictable   Unpredictable
  outcome   outcome

Figure 5 – 3

LAW-GOVERNMENT SYSTEM OPERATIONAL PREDICTABILITY

During the course of the evolution of common law consumer protection, there were periods of relative certainty about outcomes and other periods of relative uncertainty. While the law that manufacturers owed duties of care only to consumers with whom they were in privity was well established, it was a rather simple matter to ascertain the nature of the minor premise. Either the consumer purchased directly from the manufacturer or he did not. Either there was privity or there was not. Once the minor premise was established, the conclusion was not much in doubt. There was privity and thus duty, or there was no privity and thus no duty.

Then a period of some uncertainty followed. After the Thomas v. Winchester[7] case, there was an exception to the privity rule. Manufacturers owed a duty of care to ultimate consumers even in the absence of privity when the product was inherently dangerous. The problem was, What was an inherently dangerous product? The problem became more confusing and outcomes less certain when the courts confused inherently dangerous products such as guns and poison with imminently dangerous products, which are dangerous only when defective.

Even greater uncertainty followed the MacPherson case until it became generally accepted. For a while, the outcome of one's case depended on the court's perception of the importance of all these variables: the existence of absence of privity, the inherent nature of the product as dangerous or not, or the imminent danger of the product if defective, and whether distinctions between inherent and imminent were "verbal niceties" as Cardozo insisted, making them irrelevant to a solution. Once all the variables were cleared away from the decision process, relative certainty again prevailed for a time. However, there always was the lingering uncertainty related to establishing whether the manufacturer exercised or violated his duty of care to the consumer.

In the Johnson and MacPherson cases some judges made formal rational decisions while others were substantive rational. Uncertainty of outcome can depend on the inclinations of the majority and the court system relied upon. The majority proceeded one way in the federal courts and the other way in New York state courts. This uncertainty is greater at moments in legal history when the law is about to change. On these occasions, one must know that the change is imminent and in which court it is likely to take place first in order to reduce his uncertainties.

As for judges who function in a formal rational manner in some cases and in a substantive rational manner in others, there is usually some discernible pattern. A judge like Cardozo would approach contract cases in a more conservative manner than he would tort cases. Contract as a basic law for business behavior, he felt, should be constant so that business could function with a high degree of certainty. Thus he would tend to rely on formal rational decision techniques in contract cases and, as necessary, substantive rational techniques in tort cases.

One more point should be made. Some judges are more conservative than others, relying more often on formal rational techniques than their less conservative brethren. Also, some have a tendency to become more conservative as they grow older. Cardozo became conservative even in tort cases near the end of his career, and in the Palsgraf case, speaking for the court, he argued for formal rational applications of the tort doctrine of foreseeability as the New York court was resisting enlarging the duty of care by development of the proximate cause doctrine.[8] Judge Andrews was writing for a minority of the court in that case, but he provided a groundwork for later employment of proximate cause theory in New York courts.[9]

RIGHT–DUTY CERTAINTY

The individual, including the official, subject to the law–government system feels its certainties and uncertainties in terms of the degree of ambiguity of expectations others have of him and in terms of his expectations of them. In any given situation, a person's certainty as to his right–duty relationships with others is somewhere on a continuum again. (See Figure 5-4.) This time the poles are made up of absolute certainty and absolute uncertainty. And somewhere in between, moving along the continuum, is the extent of a manufacturer's duty to the consumer and the consumer's correlative right against the manufacturer, depending on how far developed is the movement from the manufacturer's immunity from product liability to his absolute liability.

0——0

Absolute   Absolute

certainty   uncertainty

Figure 5 – 4   **RIGHT–DUTY RELATIONSHIP**

SPECIFICITY

Rules

Aggravating this uncertainty and ambiguity are two inseparable phenomena—authoritative generalizations used in resolving conflicts and the circumstances of the conflicts. Highly specific generalizations produce a greater degree of certainty and less ambiguity than highly inspecific generalizations and highly inspecific circumstances. In a law–government system with the law element almost completely dominant, highly specific rules for every kind of circumstance would control right–duty relationships and the system's decision mechanisms with virtually no room for discretion or judgment by officials. In any real system, probably only small areas of human activity are capable of being subject to such highly specific rules at any given time.

Principles

Broader authoritative generalizations allowing more room for human discretion and judgment in the decision-making process can be classified as principles rather than rules. The statute of frauds requirement that any contract for the conveyance of an interest in real estate must be in writing and signed by the party to be charged can be regarded as a rule. The requirement of capacity, however, is a principle. The capacity issue must contend with the vagaries and specifics of infancy and insanity circumstances, and the capacity principle must be supported by systems of more specific rules to sort out the circumstances of each case. Greater discretion and judgment are required.

Standards

Standards represent a third form of authoritative generalization even less specific than either rules or principles. The reasonable-man standard imposed as a duty upon us all so that we do not create unreasonable risks for others is an example. At least minimally, one must conduct himself in any situation as would a reasonable man under the same or similar circumstance A variation of the standard in the area of contracts is employed to determine whether a promise was made. The objective standard—whether a reasonable man would have believed that a promise had been made to him— is often fundamental in determining whether contractual right-duty relationships exist. When such a standard is employed by an official of a law-government system, greater judgment and discretion are allowed.

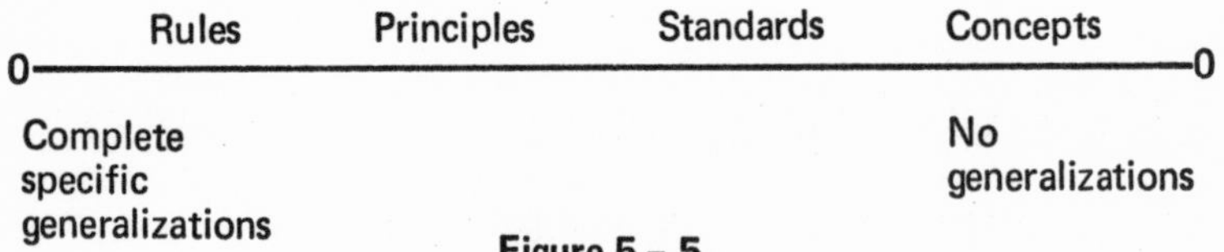

Rules	Principles	Standards	Concepts

0———————————————————————————————0

Complete specific generalizations

No generalizations

Figure 5 – 5

SPECIFICITY OF GENERALIZATION AND CIRCUMSTANCES OF EACH CASE

Concepts

The broadest authoritative generalizations are concepts. A message is lost by a communications firm due to negligence. A tort concept would permit the customer to recover consequential damages proximately resulting from the negligence. A contract concept traditionally would limit recovery to the difference between the market price of the communication service and the contract price, in which case the damage would probably be only the cost of the message. Whether the official will view the behavior of the firm as properly falling into the concept of contract and a breach of contract duty or into the concept of torts and a breach of tort duty will be an exercise of discretion of the widest latitude.[10]

COMPETING DRIVES

A law-government system will usually have competing forces operating within it to upset any momentary equilibrium in its mix of law and government elements. In addition to almost inevitable drift in the system, felt strains and senses of injustice generated by the operation of the system will produce reactions of varying kinds. These reactions can be viewed as drives to relieve strain and injustice by changing the nature and operation of the systems in some way so that obstacles to primary and instrumental goal achievement can be removed. These drives will appear in competing pairs because not everyone will have the same sense of strain or injustice arising out of the same social structure. As one dissatisfied with elements of social structure attempts to change it, another, until then satisfied, will resist the changes. As one group attempts to innovate, another attempts to retain traditional techniques and values.

It would be unrealistic to assume that all members of a group have the same status, income, wealth, education, personality, and intelligence. But for the moment assume it anyway. In the beginning all knowledge, skill, opportunity, activity, and so on are equal. Almost at once, in more complex groups, there will be a drive away from this condition of equality. Emergence of slight differences in personality, goals, ability, and interests will generate divisions of labor, which in turn will magnify differences until a time could come when hereditary status is a part of social structure. Some will be in more advantageous positions to have opportunities available, to increase their wealth, to control the rewards and punishments of the system, and to become better trained for leadership. The ultimate accomplishment of such a process would be the attainment of all power by a tyrant who would be in exclusive, unilateral control. In most groups, this would not be possible, or possible for long, because of counterforces. It would require an adequate reward and punishment system with perfect communication and appropriate identification of all group members with the tyrant. There would be no incompatible internalized reward and punishment system in any individual, and there would be complete consistency of the goals of the tyrant and the controlled. Negating all is the reality that leaders must compete for their support from nonleaders. It follows that with increasing competition, nonleaders have greater opportunities to switch their support from one leader to another in exchange for reciprocal advantages. Ultimately, competition would be so great among so many leaders that opportunity to switch support would extend to all of our fellow men. Full reciprocity would be achieved with the absolute equality of control of pure democracy and the rule of law. The drive for reciprocity always blocks the achievement of pure government.[11] (See Figure 5-6.)

Other competing drives include the drive to include discretion as one of the tools of officials, while a counterdrive is to limit exercise of discretion. A drive for certainty arising out of feelings of insecurity is countered by a drive to build flexibility into the system so that rigidity does not produce unnecessary injustices. Perhaps only another way of expressing some of the drives already mentioned is to identify the existence of competing drives for stability and change. Other competing drives are included in Figure 5-7. An interesting research possibility would be to attempt to construct a matrix of these variables, identifying the interrelated parts they played

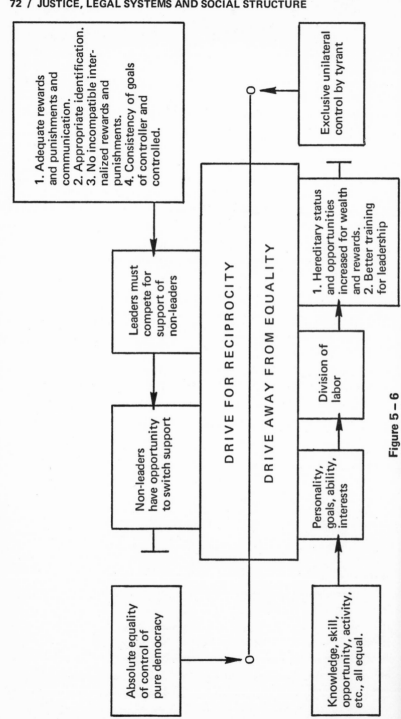

Figure 5 – 6

in establishing a particular mix of law and government elements in some area of an authority system.

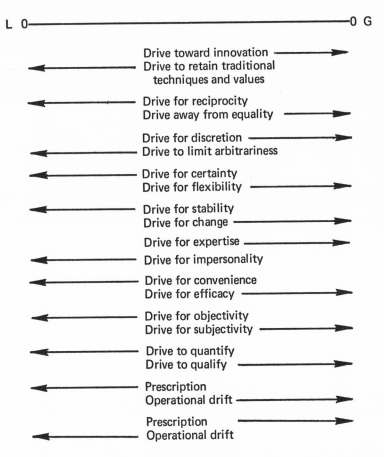

Figure 5 – 7

SOME DRIVING FORCES WITHIN THE LAW-GOVERNMENT SYSTEM

The last two items in Figure 5-7 may seem very strange. They are opposite sets of prescriptive and operational drift. Good common examples for this apparent paradox exist. The Statute of Frauds was enacted to deprive courts of jurisdiction over certain kinds of contracts unless they were in writing and signed by the party to be charged. The formal rationality of the syllogism was to block great judicial discretion, but the courts soon departed from syllogistic applications of the law and started, on a substantive rational basis, to develop exceptions. The invention of equity courts was an effort to introduce a large dose of discretionary decision making into the law-government system because the common law at the time had become very rigid. But, after a time, equity law had generated its own discretion limiting rule generalizations.

NOTES

1. The concept of law-government is a construct of Karl Llewellyn, see fn. 1, chap. 3.

2. The four decision processes for law making and finding are constructs of Max Weber. See Max Rheinstein, ed., *Max Weber, Law in Economy and Society* (Cambridge, Mass.: Harvard University Press, 1954).

3. Definitions of arbitrariness and prejudice are based on *Black's Law Dictionary* 4th ed. (St. Paul, Minn.: West Publishing Co., 1951).

4. Melville, *Moby Dick*, pp. 295-7.

5. Cadillac Motor Car Co. v. Johnson, 221F801 (1915).

6. MacPherson v. Buick Motor Co., 217 N. Y. 382, N. E. 1050 (1916).

7. Thomas and Wife v. Winchester, 6 N.Y. 397 (1852).

8. Palsgraf v. Long Island Railroad Co., 248 N.Y. 339, 162 NE 99 (1928).

9. Gardner v. Fleckenstein et al., 3 N.Y. 2d 812, (1957).

10. For such a case, refer to Judge Cardozo's opinion in behalf of the court in Kerr S.S. Co., Inc. v. Radio Corporation of America, 245 N.Y. 284, 157 N.E. 140 (1927). There the difference in damages by a contract concept and by a tort concept was the difference between $26.97 and $6,675.29. Cardozo judged the conflict to fall conceptually within the realm of contract rather than tort law. The duty breached was negligent delay in delivering a message for a fee. However, other courts in similar cases have chosen the other conceptual alternative. See Union Construction Co., v. Western Union Tel. Co. 163 Cal. 298, 311-312, 125 P. 242, (1912) and Noster v. Western Union Tel. Co., 25 F SUPP. 478, 480 (1938).

11. This paragraph and the following model are based on a discussion in Robert A. Dahl and Charles E. Lindblom, *Politics, Economics & Welfare* (New York: Harper & Row Torch Book, 1963). pp. 272-86.

6

FUNCTIONS OF LAW – GOVERNMENT

Regardless of the state of development, regardless of a group's position on the law-government continuum, and regardless of the various mixes of law and government elements within its various parts at any given time, all law-government systems perform six basic functions.[1]

THE TROUBLE CASE

Probably the one common phenomenon that induces all this official behavior is the trouble case. A trouble case involves a claim-conflict that if unresolved could impair the welfare of the group and that is distinguishable from petty strife, which is highly individual and personal in its effects. For example, a broken promise to play golf with a companion may result in some hard feelings, but strangers to the bargain are unaffected by its collapse. It's not a trouble case. But an unresolved broken promise to perform an economic exchange could affect the welfare of strangers when the members of the group are dependent on economic modes for production, exchange, and consumption of goods founded on voluntary arrangements. The first function of a law-government system is to settle trouble cases arising in all four areas of functional exigencies: economic, political, integrative, and cultural. Indeed, the act is fundamental to two of them: the political and the integrative modes.

Political behavior depends to a great extent on expediency bargaining and compromise, but those forms of behavior are not specifically referred to when the overall law-government function of settling a trouble case is the subject. They may be the criteria and means in many instances for settling trouble cases. However, the overall political function in a group is coordination and control of collective actions of the group. This coordination and control primarily anticipates, prevents, or takes care of claims-conflicts about the nature and goals of collective action—about the nature and goals of the group.

Closely related is integrative activity, which is distinguished by emphasizing the modes of creating, maintaining, and implementing norms controlling interaction among individuals and subgroups within a group. When so distinguished, attention is focused on claims—involving conflicts about the nature of social structure—and the recurrent interactions of people thought necessary to goal achievement.

What is thought necessary is dependent on the group's cultural modes of creating and maintaining values—beliefs that legitimize behavior. Some part of the trouble cases will involve claims-conflicts about behavior that really strike at beliefs about the nature and goals of the group and the recurrent interactions necessary to goal achievement.

To the extent that much of the behavior of a system is economic, it is not surprising to see great numbers of claims-conflicts viewed as trouble cases wherein the nature and goals of the group, its social structure thought necessary to goal achievement, and its beliefs are at stake. Pound's highly materialistic jural postulates and more humanistic theory of social interests seem to reflect the blend of factors that cause a conflict to be perceived as a trouble case properly to be settled by a law–government system.

CHANNELING BEHAVIOR

The values, norms, and sanctions of the law–government system reinforce the individual's organized clusters of activities, including interaction with physical, social, and cultural environment, by aiding in regularizing and inducing recurrence of interaction among two or more people. Behavior is channeled. Rational channeling should prevent disruptive trouble cases from arising. But such a result would require perfect rationality and perfect social control. Still, some preventive channeling of behavior and expectations is accomplished as a second function of a law–government system even though social control falls short of perfection and rationality. In a social context where little change is taking place, this function of law–government is commonly performed by decision techniques described as formal rational, with the law element dominating in the mix with the governmental element. In the channeling of behavior and expectations, the individual ought to be able to see the following: (1) coordination and control of collective actions of the group; (2) maintenance and implementation of norms controlling interactions among units in the system; and, both (1) and (2) to some extent affecting the modes of production, exchange, and consumption of goods and modes of creating and maintaining cultural values. The instrumental goal stability is achieved.

RECHANNELING BEHAVIOR

The activities and interests of most groups change. Strains produced within the group by insufficient social control because of the ambiguities, conflicts, discrepancies, and deprivations arising out of values, norms, and sanctions result in reactions that amount to new forms of behavior and beliefs. New behavior and beliefs are the basis for new or changing claims, which, when competing in the law-government system with recognized and protected claims and expectations, create new claims-conflicts and the need for new remedies. The old authoritative generalizations are displaced by new ones. New rules of law defining new right-duty relationships are articulated. New interactions among people are regularized. Social structure has changed to some extent. Slightly different modes of behavior in the realms of the groups' functional exigencies will have occurred. The values, norms, and sanctions of social control will have changed. The third function of the law-government system has then been performed—rechanneling of behavior. In a dynamic group, one of the functions of a law-government system must be rechanneling of behavior and expectations if the group is to survive as such and achieve the instrumental goal: progress.[2]

ALLOCATION OF AUTHORITY AND PROCEDURES

To the extent that recognized officials perform acts that can be described as coordination and control of collective activities of the group and implementation of norms governing interactions among those in the group, they perform acts of law-government. If individuals who are not recognized officials desire power and control over officials through some instrumental device such as democracy (polyarchy), then claims will be put to the law-government system for access to its political agencies and officials. If the system can accommodate such access, then acts of government will be moderated by law. A system of pure government being impossible, some access is always possible. Leaders must compete for support of nonleaders, and nonleaders have an opportunity to switch support at the minimum. From that minimum more detailed allocation of authority to persons and offices and more detailed delineations of alternative procedures are possible. The law–government system then is functioning to channel behavior and expectations of leaders and nonleaders in their interactions related to coordination and control of collective actions of the group. It is also implementing norms governing interaction among the individual and subgroup units of the society. This function (allocation of authority and procedures) can be constitutional in nature, but it is most important to see that it is primarily a specialized channeling function dependent on trouble cases involving claims-conflicts between leaders and nonleaders. It follows that to the extent that new forms of claims are displacing older recognized claims the law–government system is also performing a specialized rechanneling function. To some degree, instrumental goals of democracy, freedom, and equality may be achieved.

GOAL ACHIEVEMENT

If the law–government system is working well, it will be settling trouble cases and thereby channeling or rechanneling behavior and expectations of all members of the group, leaders and nonleaders alike, in implementation of net long-term goal achievement. Implementation of goal achievement is the fifth function of law which is derived from the other functions. It is absolutely necessary for the group to continue to survive. A group is two or more persons associated for joint activity toward achievement of common goals. The law–government system comes into existence when divergencies of urges become the basis for claim-conflicts. The groups can contend with these trouble cases by establishing an authority system. Authority-system decisions can become enforceable imperatives because of the existence of the must and supremacy elements of authority exercised purportedly on behalf of the whole group by a recognized officialdom thereby channeling or rechanneling behavior and expectations in net implementation of the group's goals.

It is advisable to view goal-achievement aspirations realistically. In more complex groups, probability of perfect achievement of all goals is low. At the least, the means for such perfect achievement are probably not at hand. Furthermore, given individual differences in interests, beliefs, priorities, attitudes, knowledge, and abilities, goal-achievement behavior conflicts with other goal-achievement behavior. The basic social processes of calculation and control for goal achievement include sociopolitical processes of polyarchy but also some hierarchy, in many areas a pricing system, and in all areas expediency bargaining and compromise.[3] Perfection is not likely. According to Dahl and Lindblom, the problems of rational calculation for control include imperfect information and communication and the number of variables in a problem and the complexity of the interrelationship of variables.[4]

To further demonstrate the difficulty in achieving all goals, Dahl and Lindblom describe these further problems.[5] There are at least four techniques of control: spontaneous, manipulative, command, and reciprocal. Which is appropriate or what blend of these is appropriate to goal achievement? Often this is determined by perceptions of the goals themselves, norms, codes, values, available sanctions, and even organization charters or constitutions which may prohibit or impair achievement. They indicate that not all possible situations nor all consequences of a control technique can be anticipated, that prescriptions may conflict, and that some prescriptions are merely intended for propaganda, morale, or public relations. Most serious is the prescription of controls that are, in fact, lacking. That is to say they contain inadequate rewards and punishments (1) for technical reasons such as lack of communications, (2) because control is, in fact, held by others with goals more consistent with those of the members of the group, (3) or because social indoctrination and habit evoke other responses. Dahl and Lindblom also indicate that one technique of control may be converted into another with unexpected results. For example, a command technique may be used by a recognized official as a basis for manipulation or as an element in bargaining with those who seek a reciprocity relationship with him.

The whole point is this: Constantly changing claims-conflicts exist because of constant experimentation with effort to get what one wants. All involved in the group are similarly involved in many of their roles, including recognized officials. Therefore, at any given time the individual will be able to perceive only the net goal achievement to date. The individual ought, further, to understand that if that given time is in the future, he as an individual will still perceive net goal achievement. But there is more. The law-government system takes claims-conflicts that are trouble cases and settles them; that is, some decision is made that sticks for the moment because of the must element, subject to the limits or control described above. Resulting behavior channeled thereby is perceived by some as goal achieving in some degree and by others as goal defeating. The sum of perceptions of goal achievement minus the sum of perceptions of goal impairment equals net goal achievement (or impairment) for the group.

If there is net goal achievement over the long term, the group is likely to endure. If there is goal impairment, either the law-government system's nature and role in the result will be changed or the group will disintegrate. Over the short term, most members of a group will probably tolerate some net goal impairment if they believe that in the long term good decision making will take place.

In any case, it should be clear that law is not a tool for instant gratification. It is a tool for the patient, incremental social problem solver. As Pound said, "I am *content to see in legal history* the record of a continually wider recognizing and satisfying of human wants . . . . a continually more efficacious social engineering."[6]

APPROPRIATE DECISION TECHNIQUES

It is not so probable that decisions are compatible with long-term goal achievement, however, without the sixth and final function of the law-government system being performed. The law-government system must function to impel appropriate decision techniques so that the process of settling trouble cases probably will channel behavior and expectations to prevent conflicts, social disruption, frictions, and waste, which block efficient goal achievement. Allocation and limitation of authority and procedures to recognized officials with a view to enabling appropriate decision techniques is a necessity. An even more highly specialized channeling of behavior of officials results. The social complexities are enormous. The education of public officials—judges, for example—is involved. They are taught traditions as to appropriate decision techniques. Methods of selecting officials must enhance the probabilities that those selected will employ appropriate decision techniques compatible with the felt needs of the times and with the prejudices shared by officials and nonofficials. Disputes rage over whether judges should be elected or appointed, with wide variations within these alternatives as well as some combinations suggested. Systems of checks and balance are created among legislative, executive, and judicial branches of a system in some groups. Appellate judicial review and administrative and legislative review procedures operate to surveil official behavior. Internal checks and balances are created. There are multimember courts with their members on the one hand restraining each other from whimsical and arbitrary decision making and on the other encouraging responsive, responsible decision making. There is circulation of leadership. Hopefully, the system can be organized so that new leaders replace old leaders slowly enough so that continuity with the past official behavior can be maintained and rapid enough so that responsiveness to changing needs is possible. In addition to all the artificial structure for impelling appropriate decision techniques, there is the effect of social-psychological determinism bearing down on the decision process resulting from the social indoctrination of the recognized officials as members of the group.

Furthermore, the system must be able to operate so that those in conflict who bring competing claims before officials for recognition can behave in ways that enlighten the decision makers to the correct choices to be made in order to enhance the social welfare. Advocacy and bargaining methods are heavily relied upon by judicial and legislative officials. Some administrative officials may also rely on independent scientific investigations, but the structure for participation therein by nonleaders is not so apparent. Courts rely heavily on the sometimes maligned advocacy system because it gives the claimants opportunities to educate the decision makers as to the nature of the claims and to the significance of their acceptance or rejection for social interests.

Basically, such claims can usually be described in terms of jural postulates. The jural postulates represent perceptions of appropriate relationships among members of a civilized society. They are assumptions about recurrent and regularized interactions—about social structure. For the law to recognize a claim and protect it by employment of enforceable imperatives is to settle a trouble case and channel behavior toward goal achievement. Of course, the channeling process may be in one of its specialized forms—rechanneling, allocation of authorities and procedures, or impelling appropriate decision techniques. The functions of law get performed. Chapter 7 develops the subject of appropriate decision techniques.

THE CONTINUUM OF FUNCTIONS

These functions can be placed in approximate positions on the law-government continuum as shown in Figure 6-1. Except for channeling, all functions have been placed to run along the continuum line, because all are performed, if they are performed at all, at any point moderately within the poles. The channeling and rechanneling functions could have been similarly placed, but instead are placed perpendicular to the continuum to locate them at points in relationship to one another and to the other functions. So placed, a statement is made about other relationships also. Compare the channeling and rechanneling locations with the locations of formal rational and substantive rational decision making, with the locations of rules, principles, standards, and concepts, and with the directions of forces driving a law-government system toward the law pole or toward the government pole. Some very important research could be done to determine the extent to which these relationships actually exist.

FUNCTIONS, POSTULATES, AND SOCIAL INTERESTS

As a law-government system functions, there tends to be a coordination between individual interests and social interests. Jural postulations arising out of claim conflicts represent expressions of individual interests. Social

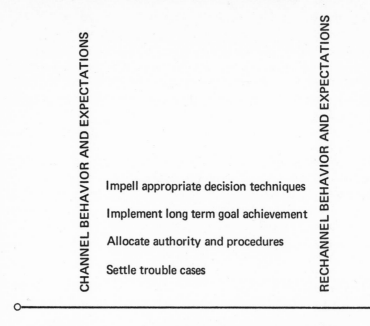

Figure 6 – 1   FUNCTIONS OF LAW-GOVERNMENT

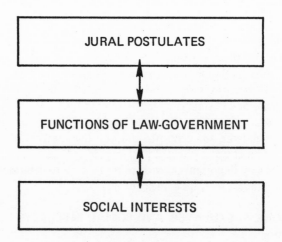

FIGURE 6 – 2   INTERRELATIONSHIP OF JURAL POSTULATES,
FUNCTIONS OF LAW-GOVERNMENT, AND SOCIAL INTERESTS

interest statements purportedly represent group utility derived from interests of individuals in the group. Claims-conflicts force the law-government
system to act. Perceptions of group interests affect the nature of the action.
The recognition and protection of some claim, demand, or expectation
based on a jural postulate and the rejection of competing ones tends to be
founded on those perceptions. The decisions of the system's officials then
tend to generate a new achievement of social interest goals as trouble cases
are settled and behavior is channeled. A direct result of the appropriate
decision technique function of law-government is the coordination of jural
postulates, the functions of law-government, and social interests as depicted
in Figure 6-2.

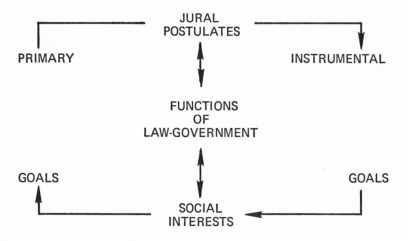

Figure 6 – 3 FUNCTIONS, POSTULATES, INTERESTS AND GOALS

FUNCTIONS, POSTULATES, INTERESTS, AND GOALS

If the primary goals and instrumental goals commonly shared by us
are related to this model, its appearance would take on the general form of
the model on sense of justice and injustice depicted in Figure 6-3.

If jural postulates are consistently and persistently individually assumed
and expressed and assumptions of social interest are articulated in a law-
government context, they must be founded on something. That foundation
is the individual's primary goals. Recognition and protection of the more
specific claims, demands, and expectations from which arise the highly
generalized jural postulates can result in enhancement of social interests.

Often these claims require behavior compatible with instrumental goals, which may be viewed as social goals upon which perceptions of social interest are founded. If social interests compatible with jural postulates are reenforced by the functions of the law-government system, then it follows that there has been some degree of primary goal achievement by at least the individuals and the group with the greatest influence over the system as a minimum and probably some new goal achievement balance for most individuals in the group.

As an example, consider again the common law evolution of consumer protection and manufacturers' product liability. The desire of a consumer to be safe in life and limb as he uses a manufactured product is based on his primary goals of continued existence and survival and physiological gratification at the least. The consumer may be assuming that manufacture, as they function, must not create unreasonable risks of loss of life or limb. If an injury caused by a negligently manufactured product befalls the consumer, he may lay claim to a remedy before the law-government system. In addition to identifying his own self-interest, the consumer may argue that a social interest is at issue. He may insist that all other members of the group have an interest in the outcome of his case. Each of them desires to maintain a minimum condition of life, which is valued as deserving of all individuals. This minimum condition requires good health, a long and productive life, and an ability to function normally employing all the bodily organs and limbs skillfully. To allow manufacturers to create unreasonable risks for life and limb is to give them license to foist on the consuming public unsafe products, which threaten the social interest in minimum standards of life deserved by all individuals. Progress toward security of life and limb with freedom from unreasonable risks would be the result of a decision favorable to the consumer, because of the channeling effect on manufacturer behavior. Manufacturers would have to take greater care than otherwise to produce safe products. The consumer's claim would then have required manufacturer behavior compatible with instrumental goals of progress, security, and freedom, which may be viewed as social goals upon which can be founded perceptions of social interest in acceptable standards of life deserved by all individuals in the group.

A social interest clearly compatible with the no-unreasonable-risk jural postulate is reenforced by the law-government system as it settles this trouble case and rechannels manufacturer behavior and consumer expectations. It follows that there has been some degree of primary goal achievement—that is, continued existence and survival, physiological gratification, and others—by consumers generally. In such a case, consumers would appear to be the subgroup with greater influence over the system. Finally, even manufacturers are individuals and consumers and would probably perceive some new goal achievement balance along with all other consumers.

FUNCTION PROCESS

The legislative, administrative, and judicial process of law–government functions in recognizing and protecting, or rejecting, claims demands and expectations may be even more succinctly summarized and viewed as the essence of appropriate decision technique. Thereafter, the process can conveniently be placed on a law-government continuum, containing the functions of law, as an elaboration of the sixth function—to impell appropriate decision techniques. The process can be simply described as a phenomenon of gradually changing claims-conflicts affording officials with perceptions of evolving social interests (social utility), which serve as criteria for resolution of conflicts.

Recognizing and protecting or rejecting
claims demands and expectations

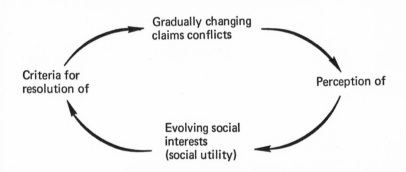

Criteria for
resolution of

Gradually changing
claims conflicts

Perception of

Evolving social
interests
(social utility)

Figure 6 – 4   **LEGISLATIVE, ADMINISTRATIVE, AND JUDICIAL PROCESSES OF LAW-GOVERNMENT FUNCTIONS.**

Figure 6–5, in effect, summarizes Chapters 5 and 6. It relates law and government on a continuum with its extremes of certainty and predictability and uncertainty and unpredictability. Simple specific circumstances, which give rise to claims-conflicts, afford opportunity for more certainty than complex nonspecific circumstances do. Simple specific rules promise more certainty and predictability of outcome than broadly generalized concepts. The degree of certainty of right–duty relationships depends on the specificity of generalization and circumstances of each case of claims-conflict. The four processes of law finding and application are spread along the continuum in their approximate places, with most of the functions of law in most systems resting on formal rational and substantive rational processes. It is necessary to the function of appropriate decision technique that claims-conflicts afford the recognized officialdom with perception of social interests which will serve as criteria for resolution. The criteria may direct

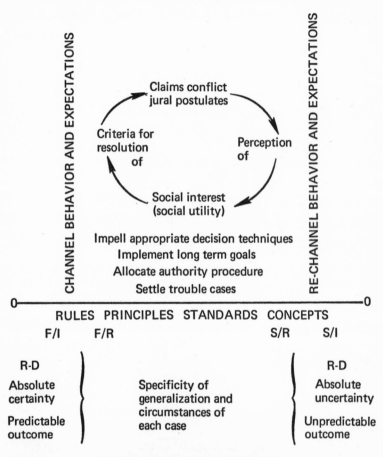

Figure 6 – 5   SUMMARY OF THE NATURE OF LAW-GOVERNMENT AND ITS FUNCTIONS

the decision maker to a formal rational process to settle a trouble case and channel behavior and expectations or it may direct him to a substantive rational process of decision making for rechanneling. If the decision making has been appropriate, net long-term goal achievement is perceived by the members of the group served by the system.

It should never be forgotten, however, that the basic part of the chart is a continuum and that the relationships depicted are not absolute. They are entirely relative. It is possible that with changed times an old law may be formal rationally applied to channel new behavior or expectations. Such is the claim made for the statute of frauds. It is said that the statute makes for sounder business planning today, though in the past it was designed to prevent courts from being used as an instrument of fraud.[7] And there are examples in the common law of substantive rational decision making to preserve well-established behavior.[8]

A serious problem with Figure 6-5 is that absolute certainty and predictability are characteristics attributed to the law pole. Yet the form of decision making nearest that pole, formal irrational, is best exemplified by techniques of randomness—that is, lotteries, coin-flipping, and trial by ordeal. No apologies are made for the paradox because at its extremes the continuum is unreal: Thus there its representations are inevitably less valid than in the midrange.

Figure 6-5 represents a hypothesis about certain approximate relationships. More research is needed in order to become comfortable with the representation.

NOTES

1. One can find many statements of the functions of law. The six listed in this chapter are intended to be basic functions performed in all law-government systems and can be found as part of the political and integrative functional exigencies of any group. They are derived from Karl Llewellyn's "The Normative, the Legal and the Law Jobs: The Problem of Juristic Method," and *The Cheyenne Way*. Other statements of law functions currently receiving much attention can be found in Harold J. Berman and William R. Greiner, *The Nature and Functions of Law* (Brooklyn, N. Y.: The Foundation Press [1966] and Robert S. Summers and Charles G. Howard, *Law: Its Nature, Functions, and Limits* (Englewood Cliffs, N.J.: Prentice-Hall, 1972).

2. The rechanneling function was explicit in the changing right-duties relationships of manufacturers and consumers described on pages 51-53 and depicted in Figure 4-1.

3. Robert A. Dahl and Charles E. Lindblom, *Politics, Economics and Welfare* (New York: Harper & Row Torch Book, 1963) pp. 171-365.

4. *Ibid.,* pp. 57-126.

5. *Ibid.,* pp. 99-109.

6. Roscoe Pound, *An Introduction to the Philosophy of Law* (New Haven, Conn.: Yale University Press, 1961), p. 47. Emphasis added.

7. Karl Llewellyn, "What Price Contract," 40 *Yale Law Journal,* 704, 747-748. (1931) For a contrary argument, see James T. Stephen, and Sir Frederick Pollock, "Section Seventeen of the Statute of Frauds," *Law Quarterly Review,* 1:1 (1885), 5-7.

8. Judge Parker, in Britton v. Turner, 6 N.H. 481, 26 Am Dec. 713 (1834), does a masterful job of substantive rational decision making to preserve the social benefits of a free enterprise system with its supporting system of contract law while he fashions a decision enabling an employee who has breached his contract promise to recover for the work he performed up to the time of the breach. The case should be read to appreciate fully how substantive rational decision making can preserve well-established social structure and law.

7

JUSTICE, LEGAL SYSTEMS, SOCIAL STRUCTURE, AND DECISION MAKING

If the group is to endure for long, its interacting units must tend to impel appropriate decision techniques enabling net goal achievement. The unit of most interest in this work is the group's law–government system. But it cannot be examined by itself. The complexity of most groups often prevents total goal achievement. One goal tends to get in the way of another in such groups so that net goal achievement is the most that can realistically be hoped for. And these complexities bear down on the law–government decision-making apparatus and personnel. The law–government system cannot contain exclusively within itself the knowledge, values, and techniques necessary to net goal achievement. Therefore, the question ought to be asked, How do such things become part of the decision-making, or problem-solving, process of a law–government system? Some of the bases for answering the question have already been developed in earlier chapters. The question to be partially explored here is, How do such things become a part of the decision maker, the recognized official?

The law–government system tends to function to transfer knowledge, values, and techniques to the recognized official for appropriate decisions if it has allocated to him authority and procedures compatible with net long-term goal achievement. The system is properly structured. But even this transfer does not represent the whole answer, because man-made structures consciously fabricated to enable rational calculation and control of social problems will be scant and at best a flimsy framework giving a sparse and approximate perception of what is expected and what can be done. There must be more.

THE INARTICULATE MAJOR PREMISE[1]

A name given to this other phenomenon controlling problem solving within the law-government system is the inarticulate major premise. The conscious or articulated part of the legal system controlling decision making is the authoritative generalization in its various forms, but primarily in the form of rules. The rule becomes the major premise in a syllogism for problem solving. It is an articulated major premise. The perceived facts of a case constitute the articulate minor premise. Then the reason of the decision maker is led to an inevitable conclusion. But the factor that controls the judgment of the recognized official in choosing one rule rather than another and causes him to perceive the facts of a case one way rather than another is referred to as the inarticulate major premise.

As Holmes said, "The felt necessity of the time, the prevalent moral and political theories, intuition of public policy, avowed or unconscious, even prejudices which judges share with their fellow men, have had a good deal more to do than the syllogism in determining the rules by which men should be governed."[2]

The official may need to employ formal rational or substantive rational (or even substantive irrational) decision making in a given case to reach the result that those in control of the legal system sense is just. But the inarticulate major premise probably controls these decision methods.

It seems to be a fact that the man in the role of the official makes his decision on the basis of far more than the "law." He may or may not be aware of all the so-called extraneous variables beyond the rules that shape his decisions, but in either case they tend to be unexpressed in his rationalizations of his decisions. Rather, his decisions seem more often to be rationalized in terms of the authority and procedures allocated to him—according to the rules. Some who object to his decisions may find fault with his rationalizing craftsmanship. Indeed, it may be faulty. But there are others who will accuse him of solving a problem according to his own sense of right and wrong—according to his own personal values—rather than the law. These accusers are aware that an inarticulate major premise may exist, but they are seriously in error about one thing: The values behind the inarticulate major premise are rarely the decision maker's unique moral code or political philosophy; rather, they are the normal code or political philosophy extant in the society or segment of the society from which the decision maker comes and of which he is a product.

THE INARTICULATE PREMISE AND JUSTICE

A sense of justice or injustice about an event is the basic stuff of the inarticulate major premise controlling the perceptions and thought processes of the decision maker in the law-government system. Of course, this does not mean that his decision will be viewed as just by all subject to the law-government system or even by a majority or even by the decision maker. It only means that some sense of justice is satisfied—either the decision maker's, or that of those in control of the decision maker and the law-government system.

The justice depicted in Chapter 1 needs an addition in order to take the inarticulate major premise into account:

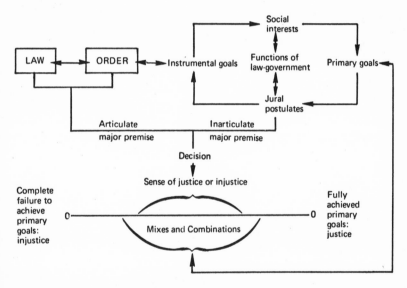

Figure 7 – 1   INARTICULATE PREMISE IN CONTEXT

The law and social policy basic to an articulate premise are not independent of an inarticulate-premise source. There is interaction in both directions. Existing notions of law and order affect the quality of the content of inarticulate-premise sources. However, the content of inarticulate-premise sources affects a decision maker's judgment of efficacious order and propitious law. But as a decision is explained—or articulated—the major and minor premises are made to appear to come directly from the law-and-order boxes with expressed social policy cast in the language of the conventional wisdom or order, whereas in reality the controlling decision premise may, though unexpressed, be derived from the right side of the model and the already felt sense of justice derived from the anticipated decision.

The desired social structure perceived necessary to achievement of instrumental and primary goals by those in control of the legal system is the raw material, along with the goals, on which the inarticulate major premise is dependent. A rule of law as an operative tool is fashioned as an articulate premise for decision making. In a well-controlled and well-planned society, the inarticulate and articulate major premises will lead the decision maker to the same conclusion in most given cases. They also will satisfy the sense of justice of those in control as they see decisions progressively moving to the right of the continuum—toward fully achieved primary goals—in Figure 7-1, which represents such a well-planned society's system. To the extent that the society is not well planned and controlled and facts of given cases refuse to fit anticipations, existential decisions, substantive rational and substantive irrational in form, controlled by the inarticulate major premise will dominate. Indeed, in allocations of authority and procedures to recognized officials, those in control may build discretion for the decision maker into the rules to take care of such cases. And where the dynamics of the society cause calculation and control in some areas to lag, such substantive rational discretionary decision making is very important in preventing the feeling of being ruled by the dead hand of the past—by unchanged, old-fashioned, inappropriate rules. But in a stable group with areas and kinds of conflict well anticipated, those in control have the opportunity to allocate authority and procedures by means of the law–government system, limiting discretion of decision makers to formal rational processes. In the dynamic situation, the inarticulate major premise impels a substantive rational process as the appropriate decision technique. In the stable situation, it impels formal rational processes.

However, one must never forget the many variables alluded to throughout this work that make the previous two statements simplistic—that is, the possible mixes and combinations of senses of justice and injustice, the complexities of social structure and law–government systems, uncertainties, specificity of generalizations and circumstances of each case, competing driving forces within the law–government system, and the rest.

Finally, it must be remembered that some sense of justice is being satisfied or some sense of injustice allayed by most decisions. Rarely, it may only be the judge's sense. More often, it is the sense of those in control of the law–government system and the officials who do their bidding. Sometimes an unjust result in one area is tolerated because of just consequences derived in another.

THE INARTICULATE PREMISE AND SOCIAL STRUCTURE

Assume that the recognized official of the law-government system is a judge sitting on a panel of judges of an appellate court. His role is made up of an identifiable cluster of activities including interaction with the group's physical, social, and cultural environment. Thereby, he participates in the modes of the functional exigencies that enable his social system to endure. His participation subjects him to the values, norms, and sanctions relevant to his role-inducing conformity and certain expectations. His interactions are recurrent and regularized because of the methods of social control, among which are the allocation to him of authority and procedures as a function of the law-government system. The resulting social structures in which he participates also cause him strain if there are ambiguities, conflicts, discrepancies, and deprivations blocking his achievement of instru-

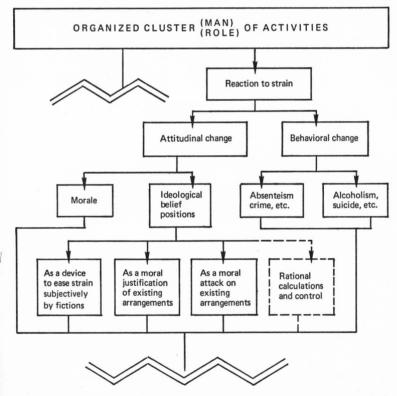

Figure 7 – 2   THE DECISION ROLE AND SOCIAL STRUCTURE
(Part 1)   AS THE INARTICULATE MAJOR PREMISE

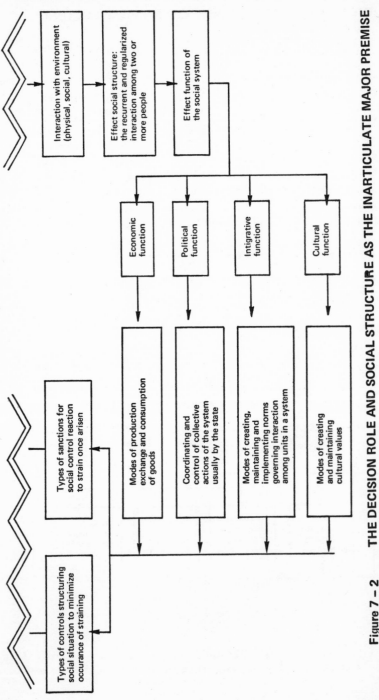

Figure 7 – 2
(Part 2)

THE DECISION ROLE AND SOCIAL STRUCTURE AS THE INARTICULATE MAJOR PREMISE

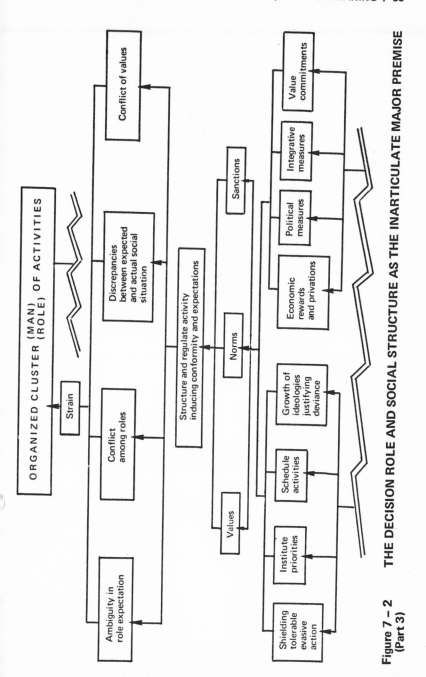

Figure 7 – 2   THE DECISION ROLE AND SOCIAL STRUCTURE AS THE INARTICULATE MAJOR PREMISE
(Part 3)

mental and primary goals. Therefore, he functions in his role according to the variety of social controls bearing upon him and as a reaction to the strains the system imposes upon him. In a given decision-making opportunity, he strives to function as social controls determine he must, or as they determine he may, or as his need to relieve feelings of strain drive him to react—or a combination of all three. Figure 7-2 is a detailed diagram of his role in the context of generalized social structure. This diagram is an elaboration of Figure 2-8. It is full of elements that rarely appear as an articulated basis for any given decision. Hence, it provides a picture of the relationship of the decision role and social structure as the inarticulate major premise.

Many devices of social control mentioned earlier can be plugged into appropriate places in Figure 7-2. As an example, mention was made earlier of the social controls on decision behavior. The manner of education of the decision maker was noted, along with methods of selection, number of decision makers participating, organizations, and process for surveilling their activity and circulation into and out of the recognized officialdom. Replacement of old decision makers with new should be rapid enough to keep decisions abreast of social change, but not so rapid that continuity with the past is lost. All those items may be seen as examples of the box identified as "structure and regulate activity inducing conformity and expectations."

A judge sensing strain because of his feelings about a case before him may act in one of four ways. First, he may develop fictions about the case, which ease his sense of strain resulting from the decision to which he feels driven by the law. His minor premise based on the facts of the case may be full of fictitious embellishments and omissions that so change his perception of the nature of the case that he can feel at peace with the outcome. C.J. Smith, writing for the Kansas Supreme Court,[4] reveals how fictions were used in an interesting case as a device to ease strain subjectively. Salesmen for the Holland Furnace Company had used fraudulent tactics to sell a furnace to Williams. The order form prepared by Holland contained these words: "This Contract Contains the Entire Agreement Between the Parties. Verbal Understandings and Agreements with Representatives Shall Not Bind the Seller Unless Set Forth Herein." The salesmen had told Williams that his furnace was defective and would permit carbon monoxide gas to escape into the house and that he and his children would be asphyxiated. This statement was a lie. Williams refused to pay for the furnace he had ordered, relying on the lie, when he discovered how he had been victimized, and Holland sued for the purchase price. The court said that the company had a right to rely on the representations of the purchaser quoted above and contained in the contract, that Holland had a constitutional right to limit the powers of its agents, and that Williams could not represent to the company that no representations had been made by the salesmen to procure the contract and then repudiate it on the ground that the salesmen had misled him. The court viewed Williams as some kind of trickster though it was Holland that had created the written contract, chosen the words the court was relying on, and trained its salesmen in fraudulent techniques. The fictions the court used were these: Williams was a trickster rather than the victim of a trick; the right to limit powers of a salesman are constitutional rights (a ridiculous fiction); Holland was deceived by Williams, this being true because Holland did not know of its salesmen's fraud—a fiction by omission because the company trained the salesmen to act as they did. Finally, the court viewed Williams as grossly negligent as well as deviant. A mechanistic decision in favor of Holland, based on strict contract interpretation, after all that, was not hard to live with, although most consumers would be shocked by the outcome.

Second, one may develop ideological beliefs as a justification of existing law and the outcome it requires in a given case. Karl Llewellyn provides an example in a discussion of the modern merits of the parol evidence rule (which was a factor in the Holland case) and the statute of frauds:

That statute is an amazing product. In it de Leon might have found his secret of perpetual youth. After two centuries and a half the statute stands, in essence better adapted to our needs than when it first was passed. By 1676 literacy (which need imply no great consistency in spelling) may well have been expected in England of such classes as would be concerned in the transactions covered by the statute's terms. Certainly, however, we had our period here in which that would hardly hold—we counted our men of affairs, in plenty, who signed by mark. But schooling has done its work. The idea which must in good part derive from the statute, that contracts at large will do well in writing, is fairly well abroad in the land. "His word is as good as his bond" contains a biting innuendo preaching caution. Meantime the modern developments of business—large units, requiring internal written records if files are to be kept straight, and officers informed, and departments coordinated, and the work of shifting personnel kept track of; the practice of confirming oral deals in writing, the use of typewriters of forms— all these confirm the policy of the statute; all these reduce the price in disappointments exacted for its benefits. The chief difficulty lies now in the very common informal verbal understandings modifying performance under a writing once made; a problem as yet inadequately solved. On the other hand, the parol evidence rule, in Wigmore's incisive phrasing the rule of integration, comes in to limit the enforceable agreement to what is incorporated in a writing, if an apparently complete writing is once made. Especially, this rule is said to eliminate any prior or contemporaneous modifying terms. As to agreements drawn under advice of counsel, the general wisdom of this is obvious; and the policy fits equally with the great bulk of agreements which are made wholly by correspondence. But in other cases—as with informal verbal modifications under the statute of frauds—the court is faced with the counter policy of recognizing the frequency with which vital terms of oral negotiations are in fact omitted from (or not reduced to) a formal writing. The course of actual decision has, in consequence, no remotest approach to the predictability the rule is supposed to achieve; a point which can hardly be too strongly stressed. Yet the net effect of the two rules together, as they work into lay practice, and viewed simply in their effects outside of litigation, is almost certainly wholesome; both in encouraging permanent trustworthy record of agreements, and in inducing care in the making of that record.[5]

Social good and wholesome effects are found in the statute of frauds and the parol evidence rule which can cause results that shock any who would identify with Williams in the Holland case. Llewellyn not so positioned, however, can tolerate the "disappointments exacted for its benefit." As to the social good the Kansas court might have perceived in its decision, it was no less than preserving the Constitution.

Third, one may develop ideological belief positions as an attack on existing law. Judge Coxe, dissenting in Cadillac Motor Car Co. v. Johnson believed that the lives and limbs of consumers ought to be more highly valued than the competing immunity from product liability of manufacture. He said:

The principles of law invoked by the defendant had their origin many years ago, when such a delicately organized machine as the modern automobile was unknown. Rules applicable to stage coaches and farm implements become archaic when applied to a machine which is capable of running with safety at the rate of 50 miles per hour . . . . it is time that the law should be changed . . . . The law should be construed to cover the conditions produced by a new and dangerous industry . . . . where the lives and limbs of human beings are at stake it is not enough for the manufacturer to assert that he . . . thought it was made of sound material.[6]

Fourth, a judge may escape the strain of his job by resorting to alcohol, absenteeism (including sleeping at the bench), inattention to cases, lazy craftsmanship in decision making, and criminal activity. He may in the last instance violate laws allocating authority and procedures to him as he decides cases. He may have been bribed or have substituted arbitrary criteria of his own for decision making. Every once in a while, a Bible-reading judge makes a practice of substituting the word of God for the word of man in deliberate disregard of the constraints imposed on him. But bribery and financial frauds are probably the principal crimes engaged in by judges. Further research on the subject should verify that hypothesis.

INDUCTIVE REASONING[7]

· Whatever the process of law finding and application in decision making, be it formal rational or substantive rational (to take the two most common forms), there are three identifiable specific thought processes involved: inductive reasoning, deductive reasoning, and judgment.

For purposes of decision making in law–government systems, inductive reasoning has as a goal the generation of a major premise and a minor premise. The major premise will be a rule, principle, standard, or concept, depending on the degree of specificity required to arrive at the decision wanted by the official. The minor premise will be the statement of the facts of the case. To arrive at each premise, the official must examine the available law and the circumstances of the case. Each is constructed out of that process.

Quickly summarizing the sweep of legal reasoning as it is commonly found in appellate courts of the American state law–government systems, one must look first at the trial court inputs. There the actual facts, to the extent that anyone who is a party to or witness in the case knows them, are presented along with the needs and goals of society claimed relevant by the parties. The trial court then determines the applicable law of the case and the applicable facts, unless there is a jury, in which case the jury determines the applicable facts. These determinations at the trial level act as a judgment filter of facts and law for the appellate system.

On appeal, the law and facts are forwarded to the appellate court in the form of a trial transcript. The transcript is a part of a class of inputs to the appellate court. Other parts of the same class of inputs include written briefs of attorneys for the litigants, in which the facts of the case and applicable laws are presented in a light most favorable to the respective parties. A third part of the same class of inputs is the oral argument each side makes to the appellate court. These arguments emphasize the legal theory, rules, applications thereof, and social policies justifying alternative findings for the litigants.

A second class of inputs sought by the appellate court in a case includes previous judicial decisions of similar claims-conflicts, statutes, and constitutions as applicable. As further input, there are other institutional constraints and sources such as rules of the court and backgrounds and knowledge of the judges.

A third class of inputs includes the perceived needs of the society, expectations of the society, and ideas about justice extant in the society. This class of input most affects the judgmental part of legal reasoning, and by virtue of that judgmental reasoning affects the nature of the inductive reasoning process, which is the subject at the moment. But with all this input, the facts of the case are classified according to legal concepts, standards, principles, and rules. Furthermore, choices are made of the relevant previous cases, statutes, interpretations, and constitutional decisions. This latter result of induction is also strongly affected by the third class of inputs which becomes a judgment filter based on the court's perceptions of the society's needs, expectations, and ideas about justice.

In the end, normative generalizations are induced from a synthesis of cases, statutes, and constitutions when applicable. Also, remember that the parts have been established and classified by induction. With the exercises of judgment, a specific normative generalization, usually a rule of law, is chosen as most applicable to the case from among all the alternatives.

DEDUCTIVE REASONING

A substantive rational process may control the fabrication of a new rule as a major premise to meet the demands for justice as perceived in the nature of facts in the case, or, employment of a well-established rule or precedent by a formal rational process may produce the wanted result. Whichever appears to be the dominant process, in either case inductive reasoning will have led the decision maker to his major and minor premises. And once they are established, the syllogism is employed. Deductive reasoning is syllogistic and appears to be scientific, making problem solving seem logical and conclusions inevitable. Its persuasive force is nearly irresistible. Deductive reasoning involves employing premises.

To elaborate, the specific normative generalization discussed in the previous section becomes the major premise for decision making. The classified facts become the minor premise. The conclusion is reached by deduction. Sometimes the conclusion causes strain for the court. Its sense of justice is not adequately satisfied. In such a case, the facts may be reworked to include fictions to relieve the strain. Or an ideological belief position is employed as a justification for the decision. Or the decision is viewed only as tentative and is scrapped before it is finally written down after a satisfactory ideological belief position has been developed, which can serve as an attack on existing law apparently responsible for the decision. Then a new or different specific normative generalization is induced which will, as employed deductively, provide a conclusion that produces little or no strain and some sense of justice. Or, being incapable of any of these attitudinal changes, the judge may simply allow the original conclusion to stand and go out and get drunk.

JUDGMENTAL REASONING

The processes of selection in constructing the major and minor premise through inductive reasoning and the evaluation of the merit of the conclusion of deductive reasoning are judgmental and based on values, emotion, bias, experience, and aspirations. Judgmental reasoning is evaluation of information, premises, and conclusions. Few decision makers will reach decisions that they and those in control of the law-government system do not want. Social control of the attitude and behavior of the official is an important part of the judgmental reasoning process. If human life and welfare are highly valued and a personal injury case involves a highly impersonal wealthy business organization as an antagonist, a court may see only facts qualifying an employee for a workman's compensation remedy. In one case the circumstances were that an employer furnished transportation for an employee to reach his job. The employee was injured while availing himself of the transportation. The court concluded that the employee was within the scope of his employment when injured and was unconcerned about the presence or absence of negligence by the employer.[8] In another case an employer also furnished transportation for an employee to reach his job. That employee was also injured while availing himself of the transportation. Virtually the same court did not see facts qualifying the employee for a workman's compensation remedy. It concluded he was not within the scope of his employment when injured and in order to recover damages he had to resort to a claim that the employer was negligent.[9] But when the employer's negligence has clearly caused the employee's injuries it is to the employee's advantage to recover on a tort theory because of the absence of statutory limits on recovery imposed in workman's compensation legislation.

Two such cases may appear inconsistent on the surface, but in each case the same inarticulate major premise is controlling the judgmental reasoning process. Placing the employee within the scope of his employment assures him a recovery under workman's compensation schedules, even in the absence of negligence by the employer. Placing him outside the scope of his employment in the second example, involving virtually the same facts, assures him the possibility of a maximum recovery under tort law.

A careful examination of the elements of the decision processes in these examples can help one articulate the inarticulate premise. In each case, the parties bring to the decision makers their legal theories and perceptions of reality.

Case One

Plaintiff:

Legal theory (major premise)
   Workman's compensation law (One injured while within the scope of his employment is entitled to a workman's compensation award without regard to the absence of negligence on the part of the employer.)
Perception of reality (minor premise)
   Plaintiff was injured while within the scope of his employment.
Conclusion
   Plaintiff is entitled to a workman's compensation award.

Defendant:

Legal theory (major premise)
   Tort law of negligence (An employee injured outside the scope of his employment is barred from recovery under workman's compensation. He can only recover on tort theory if the defendant has no defenses.)
Perception of reality (minor premise)
   Plaintiff was outside the scope of his employment when injured.
Conclusion
   Plaintiff is barred from recovery under workman's compensation law.
So far these positions can be represented by Figure 7–3:

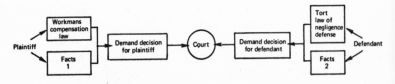

1. Facts justifying conclusion plaintiff within scope of employment when injured.

2. Facts justifying conclusion plaintiff outside scope of employment when injured.

Figure 7 – 3

The decision makers may accept the premises of the plaintiff or the defendant, or (not likely in this case) develop some of their own.

Case Two

Plaintiff:

Legal theory (major premise)
    Tort law of negligence (an employee injured outside the scope of his
    employment is barred from recovery under workman's compensation
    and must resort to tort negligence theory, subject to all defenses for
    recovery.)
Perception of reality (minor premise)
    Plaintiff was injured by defendant's negligence while outside the
    scope of employment.
Conclusion
    Plaintiff is barred from recovery under workman's compensation
    but may recover for negligence.

Defendant:

Legal theory (major premise)
    Workman's compensation law (One injured within the scope of his
    employment is entitled only to a workman's compensation award.)
Perception of reality (minor premise)
    Plaintiff was injured within the scope of his employment.
Conclusion
    Plaintiff is limited to a workman's compensation remedy.
So far, this case can be represented by Figure 7-4.

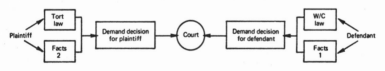

Figure 7 – 4

Clearly, each party argues for acceptance of the major and minor premises
that are to his advantage. The problem is to ascertain the self-interest of the
court that will force it to choose one set of premises.

Reference to functions, postulates, interests and goals, pp. 83-84, and to
postulates, interests and goals, pp. 55-57 reminds one of the relationship of
jural postulates, social interests, and the function of law and goals, and provides a map to guide the search for the inarticulate major premises and justice in these cases. In each instance, a trouble case will be settled, and
hopefully, channeling of behavior and expectations in the service of better

net goal achievement will follow. The specifics of these elements are better understood if the legal theories of the plaintiffs and defendants can be matched to jural postulates.

In each case, the plaintiff's primary goals are very basic: He wants to continue to survive and to achieve fundamental physiological gratifications. A decision in his favor will, to some extent, provide the means. He wants to control and use those things he has and enjoys without unreasonable risk caused by others or by the system within which he functions.

The defendant also wants to control and use those things he has and enjoys, free of unreasonable claims by others. The defendant wants his business and his profits—not unnatural in an economic system with elements of free enterprise. The defendant basically is trying to protect his pocketbook, and the plaintiff is trying to protect life and limb. The choice is not unlike the choice in the consumer protection cases discussed earlier.

The plaintiff's interests are well matched with the social interest of promotion of individual life according to standards extant in the community, whereas the defendant's interests are better identified with the social interest in security of social institutions such as the marketplace and profit in a free enterprise system.

Decisions in these cases will enhance one set of individual goals, jural postulates, and correlative social interests at the expense of the other—hence net goal achievement. The inarticulate major premise is fabricated out of a set of jural postulates, social interests, and functions of law. The inarticulate major premise bore down heavily on the court in these two cases. Although in the past it had forced decisions in favor of free markets, profit, and private property even at the expense of life and limb, at the time of these decisions society had moved to a condition of greater concern for life and limb and was producing judicial decision makers sharing that concern. On that basis, the decisions were consistent.

A representation of the relationship of the inarticulate major premise to the decision process and to the other variables discussed in this section is given in Figure 7-5.

If the decision goes the other way, the weight of the diagram is shifted to the other side and the inarticulate major premise has its source on the other side. If the decision involves alternative law and facts, it may be because the court is affected by an inarticulate major premise with sources in the elements of both parties' cases and/or with additional elements.

The process is elaborated in Figure 7-6.

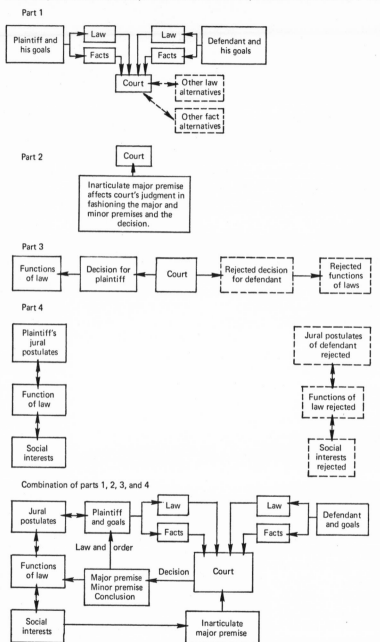

Figure 7 – 5
CASE CONTEXT OF AN INARTICULATE MAJOR PREMISE

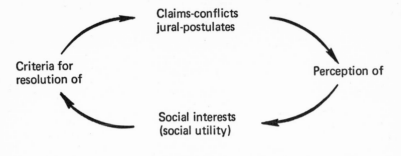

Figure 7 – 6   **APPROPRIATE DECISION TECHNIQUE**

STYLES OF DECISION EXPRESSION

Sometimes styles of decision expression are mistaken for the fundamental inductive, deductive, and all-important judgmental reasoning processes of decision makers. Usually, when a decision maker begins to announce his decision, the decision has already been made, and any elaboration of how he arrived at the decision is after the fact. Such elaboration may or may not be accurate. Even if he flipped a coin to reach his decision, unless flipping coins was the allocated procedure in such cases, the decision maker must cast his explanation in a style acceptable to those who allocated his authority to him. Tradition has presented us with certain styles for explaining decisions. They are expected by all and are carefully taught to the decision makers in schools of law and other institutions for training them.

Although these styles may often obscure the real reasons for a decision, they are of value because the decision maker must not have acted so arbitrarily that he cannot rationalize according to one or more of the style forms. Thus they become constraints—part of the allocated procedure for decision making and stuff susceptible to surveillance by all who wish to exercise some immediate control over the recognized officialdom of the law-government system. They are part of the class-two inputs referred to in the inductive reasoning section designated as other institutional constraints and sources. They appear early in the reasoning process because all craft-wise judges have in mind as they go about reaching a decision that their explanations must be cast in a traditional and acceptable style.

More positively stated, the inevitability of the styles may compel decision processes of induction, deduction, and judgment which are appropriate to goal achievement. There are four styles—meaning of the rule, purpose of the rule, precedent and analogy, and social policy. The meaning of the rule

approach to decision making is dominantly formal rational and is appropriate in conflict resolution where stability is the important instrumental goal
to be served. The purpose of the rule approach is also formal rational, but
the government component in the law–government continuum is a greater
part of the mix with the law component than in the meaning of the rule
style.

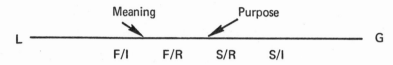

Figure 7 – 7
RULES & LAW-GOVERNMENT MIXES

Precedent and analogy are apparently dominated by a large amount of
inductive reasoning, but the end result is a rule which may be either well
established or new. If well established, then it is susceptible to application
by the meaning of the rule approach or the purpose of the rule approach.
The social policy style relies heavily on expressions of social values and goals
justifying the decision and may supplement any of the other styles or be the
basis for substantive rational innovation. Paradoxically, it can also justify
the formalities for formal irrational techniques. The social policy of equal
treatment of potential draftees for the military service justified resorting to
a lottery as a selection method. Drawing numbers from a fish bowl is formal
irrational decision making in determining who will serve in the military.

Meaning of the Rule

A strict construction of a rule of law, including strict application, is the
essence of the meaning of the rule style of decision explanation. The decision maker has arrived at his decision and can best rationalize it by a mechanistic application of law. For example, in a famous case authored by
Justice Holmes, an airplane had been stolen.[10] The thief was convicted of
violating a statute forbidding interstate transportation of a stolen motor
vehicle. Holmes overturned the trial court verdict on the theory that the
statute did not specifically identify an airplane as a motor vehicle although
it included examples of other kinds of motor vehicles. The decision turning
on a technicality looks legalistic and therefore artificial. It is not the decision in this case that is artificial but only the style of its expression.

Holmes was concerned with fair play for defendants. Fair play includes
drafting legislation so that one can know in advance whether his deeds are
proscribed by criminal statute. His concern was the balance of power between the individual and the state and that the state not be able to act

arbitrarily. He feared police use of a loosely drawn statute in a substantive irrational way to the surprise of an individual who could not in advance properly channel his behavior according to the law. In reality it was a fundamental polyarchic political philosophy of law–government that dominated Holmes' decision making in this case. But he could explain the result of his decision making by a strict interpretation of a criminal statute limited to the meaning of its words. Though he appeared highly mechanistic, his behavior is supported by a common law tradition of strict interpretation of criminal statute, which exists because of historical concern for the fairness of the warning criminal law ought to give.

Purpose of the Rule

In the case just alluded to, strict constructionism is not employed in the service of law and order as that phrase is commonly understood today. The law and order advocate must surely feel uncomfortable to see strict constructionism used as it was. He might be surprised to learn that liberal interpretation of law better suited his notions of the appropriate way to deal with criminals. The dissenters on the court argued that the purpose of the statute was to prevent theft and interstate transportation of motor vehicles, even the airplane, although it was not included specifically. That was the purpose of the rule even though the legislature did not think of it.

For the dissenting justices, the concern must have been to employ the law to protect certain interests, notably the institution of private property, from deviant behavior posing a basic threat to it. After all, the institution of private property (along with contract) constitutes the legal foundation for our highly successful economic system, which in its own way also promotes a political philosophy of individualism. The best way available to these justices to protect private property was to seize the opportunity provided by this case and employ the purpose of the rule style to explain their dissenting decision.

Precedent and Analogy

It is popular to believe that *stare decises* requires a peculiar kind of thinking useful only to lawyers. "I told him it was law logic—an artificial system of reasoning, exclusively used in courts of justice, but good for nothing else." John Quincy Adams' statement refers to the style of decision rationalizing employing precedent and analogy. The statement is unfair to anyone who uses experience as a guide to decision making in any walk of life. However, a formalization of reliance on experience as found in common-law systems can have its shortcomings. Holmes was to the point when he said, "It is revolting to have no better reason for a rule than that it was laid down in the time of Henry IV. It is still more revolting if the grounds upon which it was laid down have vanished long since and the rule simply persists from blind imitation of the past." But one must be aware that people in all walks of life persist in blind imitation of the past as they rely on experience to attempt to solve their problems. There is truth for all of us in William Scott's statement that "a precedent embalms a principle."

Basically, precedent is successful experience repeated again and again with aspirations for further successes. It is a reasonable way to solve one's problems whether one is a recognized official or not. Use of precedent, too, tends to cloud the picture of real decision making. We all have thousands of past experiences and thus many precedents to draw upon by induction and to evaluate by judgment. It is in the judging that the real decision is made. At that point, values, goals, and biases are determining the outcome. In the end, the relevant precedent is probably recognized on the basis of its compatibility with the decision already arrived at.

Analogy is employed in the absence of direct experience. It is commonly used in argumentation by those who have already made up their minds.[11] The written decision of a court is often an argument cast in the style of a decision explanation. The technique is, in the absence of precedent or other guiding rules, to resort to hypothetical experience applied to a hypothetical problem so as to produce what most would agree is a reasonable result. Then one identifies the similarities of the real problem with the hypothetical and justifies his similar conclusions. It is the rare case when competing analogies cannot be generated by those desiring a different solution. Precedent and analogy are useful and are employed by us all even as we employ purpose of the rule and meaning of the rule techniques to justify our decisions.

Social Policy

Precedent and analogy may be employed in conjunction with meaning of the rule or purpose of the rule styles. So too may social policy, which may be employed compatibly with precedent and analogy. A decision rationalization in elaborate form may contain elements of three of the four styles. Meaning of the rule and purpose of the rule styles tend to exclude one another from the same text, though not always.

Social policy style brings to the surface more of the actual decision process than the others. The social values, primary and instrumental goals, social utility, and commonly shared senses of justice that affect judgment in the reasoning process may be revealed as reasons for the minor and major premise results of the induction and deductive processes. For example,

Justice Cardoza explained one of his decisions as dependent only on social policy grounds.[12] He was confronted with a case in which a boy standing over a public waterway on a plank attached to private property was killed because of an unsafe utility pole negligently maintained by the property owner. Two laws seemed to control. One required private-property owners to abstain from negligent behavior or actions that create or allow a dangerous condition on his property to harm one on a public way where he had a right to be. The other recognized that a property owner owed no duty of care to a trespasser. Was the boy a trespasser or on a public way? Cardoza held the boy to be on public way and the property owner to be liable as a matter of public policy and justice.

Finally, it should be recognized that public policies can compete and that no particular decision is inevitable when public policy is relied upon. For example, in the Holmes case, public-policy arguments for fair treatment of individuals by the state and for protection of the institution of private property could have been made.

NOTES

1. The inarticulate major premise is a formulation of Oliver W. Holmes, Jr. See Lochner v. New York 198 U.S. 45 at page 75 (1904) and Adeins v. Children's Hospital, 261 U.S. 525, 567 (1923). There is an interesting discussion of the inarticulate major premise in James N. Davis et al., Society and the Law (New York: Free Press, 1962), pp. 126–130.

2. Oliver W. Holmes, Jr., The Common Law (Boston: Beacon Press 1963), p. 1.

3. This chart summarizes material throughout Neil J. Smelser, The Sociology of Economic Life (Englewood Cliffs, N.J.: Prentice-Hall 1963) and is an elaboration of Figure 2–8.

4. Holland Furnace Co. v. Williams, 179 KAN. 321, 295 p. 672 (1956).

5. Karl Llewellyn, "What Price Contract," 40 Yale Law Journal 704, 747-8 (1931).

6. 221 F. 801

7. Inductive, deductive, and judgmental reasoning processes and institutional constraints on decision makers described hereafter are based in part on theories and observations of Karl Llewellyn, The Common Law Tradition (Boston: Little Brown, 1960).

8. Littler v. George A. Fuller Co., 223 N.Y. 369, 119 N.E. 554 (1918).

9. Tallon v. Interborough Rapid Transit Co., 323 N.Y. 410, 134 N.E. 327 (1922).

10. McBoyle v. United States, 283 U.S. 25, 51 S.Cr. 340 (1931).

11. Review Herman Melville's chapter on Fast-Fish and Loose-Fish, pages 21-23 and 63-65 herein. Notice the analogy drawn between the whale and the lady.

12. Hynes v. N.Y. Central Railroad Co., 231 N.Y. 229, 131 N.E. 898 (1921).

8

CASE DECISIONS AND JUSTICE

This work is not a casebook, but the inclusion of case material is not inappropriate. In this section, a case is set out to give the reader an opportunity to feel some mix of senses of justice and injustice concerning its events, its conflict, and a law-government system interaction therewith. One may want to analyze this case and his feelings about it using the hypotheses and constructs of this work. Then a hypothetical fact situation is set up, and two possible decisions are offered that incorporate some of these hypotheses and constructs. One may want to imagine his own decision in detail and compare it with the two offerings. Finally the facts of a real case, including the verdict of the trial jury, but not including an appellate court decision, are recounted. If the reader can analyze the facts and develop and express a position by employing the hypotheses and constructs of this work with some feeling of confidence and satisfaction in the result, then the goal of this work has been achieved.

REGINA v. DUDLEY AND STEPHENS[1]

Indictment for the murder of Richard Parker on the high seas within the jurisdiction of the Admiralty.

At the trial before Huddleston, B., at the Devon and Cornwall Winter Assizes, November 7, 1884, the jury, at the suggestion of the learned judge, found the facts of the case in a special verdict which stated "that on July 5, 1884, the prisoners, Thomas Dudley and Edward Stephens, with one Brooks, all able-bodied English seamen, and the deceased also an English boy, between seventeen and eighteen years of age, the crew of an English yacht, a registered English vessel, were cast away in a storm on the high seas 1600 miles from the Cape of Good Hope, and were compelled to put into an open boat belonging to the said yacht. That in this boat they had no supply of water and no supply of food, except two 1 lb. tins of turnips, and for three days they had nothing else to subsist upon. That on the fourth day they caught a small turtle, upon which they subsisted for a few days, and this was the only food they had up to the twentieth day when the act now in question was committed. That on the twelfth day remains of the turtle were entirely consumed, and for the next eight days they had nothing to eat. That they had no fresh water, except such rain as they from time to time caught in their oilskin capes. That the boat was drifting on the ocean, and was probably more than 1000 miles away from land. That on the eighteenth day, when they had been seven days without food and five without water, the prisoners spoke to Brooks as to what should be done if no succour came, and suggested that some one should be sacrificed to save the rest, but Brooks dissented, and the boy, to whom they were understood to refer, was not consulted. That on the 24th of July, the day before the act now in question, the prisoner Dudley proposed to Stephens and Brooks that lots should be cast who should be put to death to save the rest, but Brooks refused to consent, and it was not put to the boy, and in point of fact there was no drawing of lots. That on that day the prisoners spoke of their having families, and suggested it would be better to kill the boy that their lives should be saved, and Dudley proposed that if there was no vessel in sight by the morrow morning the boy should be killed. That next day, the 25th of July, no vessel appearing, Dudley told Brooks that he had better go and have a sleep, and made signs to Stephens and Brooks that the boy had better be killed. The prisoner Stephens agreed to the act, but Brooks dissented from it. That the boy was then lying at the bottom of the boat quite helpless, and extremely weakened by famine and by drinking sea water, and unable to make any resistance, nor did he ever assent to his being killed. The prisoner Dudley offered a prayer asking forgiveness for them all if either of them should be tempted to commit a rash act, and that their souls might be saved. That Dudley, with the assent of Stephens went to the boy, and telling him that his time was come, put a knife into his throat and killed him then and there; that the three men fed upon the body and blood of the boy for four days; that on the fourth day after the act had been committed the boat was picked up by a passing vessel, and the prisoners were rescued, still alive, but in the lowest state of prostration. That they were carried to the port of Falmouth, and committed for trial at Exeter. That if the men had not fed upon the body of the boy they would probably not have survived to be so picked up and rescued, but would within the four days have died of famine. That the boy, being in a much weaker condition, was likely to have died before them. That at the time of the act in question there was no sail in sight, nor any reasonable prospect of relief. That under these circumstances there appeared to the prisoners every probability that unless they then fed or very soon fed upon the boy or one of themselves they would die of starvation. That there was no appreciable chance of saving life except by killing some one for the others to eat. That assuming any necessity to kill anybody, there was no greater necessity for killing the boy than any of the other three men. But whether upon the whole matter by the jurors found the killing of Richard Parker by Dudley and Stephens by felony and murder the jurors are ignorant, and pray the advice of the Court thereupon, and if upon the whole matter the Court shall be of opinion that the killing of Richard Parker be felony and murder, then the jurors say that Dudley and Stephens were each guilty of felony and murder as alleged in the indictment."

Dec. 9. The judgment of the Court (Lord Coleridge, C.J., Grove and Denman, J.J., Pollock and Huddleston, B.B.) was delivered by Lord Coleridge, C.J. ... There remains to be considered the real question in the case—whether killing under the circumstances set forth in the verdict be or be not murder. The contention that it could be anything else was, to the minds of us all, both new and strange, and we stopped the Attorney General in his negative argument in order that we might hear what could be said in support of a proposition which appeared to us to be at once dangerous, immoral, and opposed to all legal principle and analogy. All, no doubt, that can be said has been urged before us, and we are now to consider and determine what it amounts to. First it is said that it follows from various definitions of murder in books of authority, which definitions imply, if they do not state, the doctrine, that in order to save your own life you may lawfully take away the life of another, when that other is neither attempting nor threatening yours, nor is guilty of any illegal act whatever toward you or anyone else. But if these definitions be looked at they will not be found to sustain this contention. The earliest in point of date is the passage cited to us from Bracton, who lived in the reign of Henry III. ... But in the very passage as to necessity, on which reliance has been placed, it is clear that Bracton is speaking of necessity in the ordinary sense—the repelling by violence, violence justified so far as it was necessary for the object, any illegal violence used towards oneself. If, says Bracton, the necessity be "evitabilis, et evadere posse absque occisione, tunc erit reus homicidii"— words which shew clearly that he is thinking of physical danger from which *escape* may be possible, and that "inevitabilis necessitas" of which he speaks as justifying homicide is a necessity of the same nature.

It is, if possible, yet clearer that the doctrine contended for receives no support from the great authority of Lord Hale. It is plain that in his view the necessity which justified homicide is that only which has always been and is now considered a justification. "In all these cases of homicide by necessity," says he, "as in pursuit of a felon, in killing him that assaults to rob, or comes to burn or break a house, or the like, which are in themselves no felony." (Hale's Pleas of the Crown, I p. 491.) Again, he says that "the necessity which justifies homicide is of two kinds: (1) the necessity which is of a private nature; (2) the necessity which relates to the public justice and safety. The latter is that necessity which relates to the public justice and safety. The former is that necessity which obligeth a man to his own defence and safeguard, and this takes in these inquires:—(1) What may be done for the safeguard of a man's own life"; and then follow three other heads not necessary to pursue. The Lord Hale proceeds:—"As touching the first of these— viz., homicide in defence of a man's own life, which is usually styled *se defendendo.*" It is not possible to use words more clear to show that Lord Hale regarded the private necessity which justified, and alone justified, the taking the life of another for the safeguard of one's own to be what is commonly called "self-defence." (Hale's Pleas of the Crown, I p. 478.)

But, if this could be even doubtful upon Lord Hales' words, Lord Hale himself has made it clear. For in the chapter in which he deals with the exemption created by compulsion or necessity he thus expresses himself:— "If a man be desperately assaulted and in peril of death, and cannot otherwise escape unless, to satisfy his assailant's fury, he will kill an innocent person then present, the fear and actual force will not acquit him of the crime and punishment of murder, if he commit the fact, for he ought rather to die himself than kill an innocent; but if he cannot otherwise save his own life the law permits him in his own defence to kill the assailant, for by the violence of the assault, and the offence committed upon him by the assailant himself, the law of nature, and necessity, hath made him his own protector *cum debito moderamine inculpatae tutelae."* (Hale's Pleas of the Crown, I p. 51.)

But further still, Lord Hale in the following chapter deals with the position asserted by the casuists, and sanctioned, as he says by Grotius and Puffendorf, that in a case of extreme necessity, either of hunger or clothing, "theft is no theft, or at least not punishable as theft, as some even of our own lawyers have asserted the same." "But," says Lord Hale, "I take it that here in England, that rule, at least by the laws of England, is false; and therefore, if a person, being under necessity for want of victuals or clothes, shall upon that account clandestinely and *animo furandi* steal another man's goods, it is felony, and a crime by the laws of England punishable with death." (Hale, Pleas of the Crown, I p. 54.) If, therefore, Lord Hale is clear—as he is—that extreme necessity of hunger does not justify larceny, what would he have said to the doctrine that it justified murder?

It is satisfactory to find that another great authority, second, probably, only to Lord Hale, speaks with the same unhesitating clearness on this matter. Sir Michael Foster, in the 3rd Chapter of his Discourse on Homicide, deals with the subject of "homicide founded in necessity"; and the whole chapter implies, and is insensible unless it does imply, that in the view of Sir Michael Foster "necessity and self-defence" (which he defines as "opposing force to force even to the death") are convertible terms. There is no hint, no trace, of doctrine now contended for; the whole reasoning of the chapter is entirely inconsistent with it.

In East's Pleas of the Crown (i. 271) the whole chapter on homicide by necessity is taken up with an elaborate discussion of the limits within which necessity in Sir Michael Foster's sense (given above) of self-defence is a justification of excuse for homicide. There is a short section at the end very generally and very doubtfully expressed, in which the only instance discussed is the well-known one of two shipwrecked men on a plank able to sustain only one of them, and the conclusion is left by Sir Edward East entirely undetermined.

What is true of Sir Edward East is true also of Mr. Serjeant Hawkins. The whole of his chapter on justifiable homicide assumes that the only justifiable homicide of a private nature is the defence against force of a man's person, house, or goods. In the 26th section we find again the case of two shipwrecked men and the single plank, with the significant expression from a careful writer, "It is said to be justifiable." So, too, Dalton c. 150, clearly considers necessity and self-defence in Sir Michael Foster's sense of that expression, to be convertible terms, though he prints without comment Lord Bacon's instance of the two men on one plank as a quotation from Lord Bacon, adding nothing whatever to it of his own. And there is a remarkable passage at page 229, in which he says that even in the case of a murderous assault upon a man, yet before he may take the life of the man who assaults him even in self-defence, "*cuncta prius tentanda.*"

The passage in Staundforde, on which almost the whole of the dicta we have been considering are built, when it comes to be examined, does not warrant the conclusion which has been derived from it. The necessity to justify homicide must be, he says inevitable, and the example which he gives to illustrate his meaning is the very same which has just been cited from Dalton, shewing that the necessity he was speaking of was a physical necessity, and the self-defence a defence against physical violence. Russell merely repeats the language of the old text-books, and adds no new authority, nor any fresh considerations. . . .

The one real authority of former time is Lord Bacon, who, in his commentary on the maxim, "*necessitas induct privilegium quoad jura privata,*" lays down the law as follows:—"Necessity carrieth a privilege in itself. Necessity is of three sorts—necessity of conservation of life, necessity of obedience, and necessity of the act of God or of a stranger. First of conservation of life: if a man steal viands to satisfy his present hunger, this is no felony nor larceny. So if divers be in danger of drowning by the casting away of some boat or barge, and one of them gets to some plank, or on the boat's side to keep himself above water, and another to save his life thrust him from it, whereby he is drowned, this is neither *se defendendo* nor by misadventure, but justifiable." On this it is to be observed that Lord Bacon's proposition that stealing to satisfy hunger is no larceny is hardly supported by Staundforde, whom he cites for it, and is expressly contradicted by Lord Hale in the passage already cited. And for the proposition as to the plank or boat, it is said to be derived from the canonists. At any rate he cites no authority for it, and it must stand upon his own. Lord Bacon was great even as a lawyer; but it is permissible to much smaller men, relying upon principle and on the authority of others, the equals and even the superiors of Lord Bacon as lawyers, to question the soundness of his dictum. There are many conceivable states of things in which it might possibly be true, but if Lord Bacon meant to lay down the broad proposition that a man may save his life by killing, if necessary, an innocent and unoffending neighbor, it certainly is not law at the present day . . . .

Now, except for the purpose of testing how far the conservation of a man's own life is in all cases and under all circumstances an absolute, unqualified, and paramount duty, we exclude from our consideration all the incidents of war. We are dealing with a case of private homicide, not one imposed upon men in the service of their Sovereign and in the defence of their country. Now it is admitted that the deliberate killing of this unoffending and unresisting boy was clearly murder, unless the killing can be justified by some well-recognized excuse admitted by the law. It is further admitted that there was in this case no such excuse, unless the killing was justified by what has been called "necessity." But the temptation to the act which existed here was not what the law has ever called necessity. Nor is this to be regretted. Though law and morality are not the same, and many things may be immoral which are not necessarily illegal, yet the absolute divorce of law from morality would be of fatal consequence; and such divorce would follow if the temptation to murder in this case were to be held by law an absolute defence of it. It is not so. To preserve one's life is generally speaking a duty, but it may be plainest and the highest duty to sacrifice it. War is full of instances in which it is a man's duty not to live, but to die. The duty, in case of shipwreck, of a captain to his crew, of the crew to the passengers, of soldiers to women and children, as in the noble case of the *Birkenhead;* these duties impose on men the moral necessity, not of the preservation, but of the sacrifice of their lives for others, from which in no country, least of all, it is to be hoped, in England, will men ever shrink, as indeed, they have not shrunk. It is not correct, therefore, to say that there is any absolute or unqualified necessity to preserve one's life. *"Necesse est ut eam, non ut vivam,"* is a saying of a Roman officer quoted by Lord Bacon himself with high eulogy in the very chapter on necessity to which so much reference has been made. It would be a very easy and cheap display of commonplace learning to quote from Greek and Latin authors, from Horace, from Juvenal, from Cicero, from Euripides, passage after passage, in which the duty of dying for others has been laid down in glowing and emphatic language as resulting from the principles of heathen ethics; it is enough in a Christian country to remind ourselves of the Great Example whom we profess to follow. It is not needful to point out the awful danger of admitting the principle which has been contended for. Who is to be the judge of this sort of necessity? By what measure is the comparative value of lives to be measured? Is it to be strength, or intellect, or what? It is plain that the principle leaves to him who is to profit by it to determine the necessity which will justify him in deliberately taking another's life to save his own. In this case the weakest, the youngest, the most unresisting, was chosen. Was it more necessary to kill him than one of the grown men? The answer must be "No:—

"So spake the Fiend, and with necessity,
The tyrant's plea, excused his devilish deeds."
It is not suggested that in this particular case the deeds were "devilish," but it is quite plain that such a principle once admitted might be made the legal cloak for unbridled passion and atrocious crime. There is no safe path for judges to tread but to ascertain the law to the best of their ability and to declare it according to their judgment; and if in any case the law appears to be too severe on individuals, to leave it to the Sovereign to exercise that prerogative of mercy which the Constitution has intrusted to the hands fittest to dispense it.

It must not be supposed that in refusing to admit temptation to be an excuse for crime it is forgotten how terrible the temptation was; how awful the suffering; how hard in such trials to keep the judgment straight and the conduct pure. We are often compelled to set up standards we cannot reach ourselves, and to lay down rules which we could not ourselves satisfy, but a man has no right to declare temptation to be an excuse, though he might himself have yielded to it, nor allow compassion for the criminal to change or weaken in any manner the legal definition of the crime. It is therefore our duty to declare that the prisoners' act in this case was wilful murder, that the facts as stated in the verdict are no legal justification of the homicide; and to say that in our unanimous opinion the prisoners are upon this special verdict guilty of murder.

THE CASE OF THE SPELUNCEAN EXPLORERS[2]

The defendants, having been indicted for the crime of murder, were convicted and sentenced to be hanged by the Court of General Instances of the County of Stowfield. They bring a petition of error before this Court. The facts sufficiently appear in the opinion of the Chief Justice.

Truepenny, C.J. The four defendants are members of the Speluncean Society, an organization of amateurs interested in the exploration of caves. In the company of Roger Whetmore, then also a member of the Society, they penetrated into the interior of a limestone cavern of the type found in the Central Plateau of this Commonwealth. While they were in a position remote from the entrance to the cave, a landslide occurred. Heavy boulders fell in such a manner as to block completely the only known opening to the cave. When the men discovered their predicament they settled themselves near the obstructed entrance to wait until a rescue party should remove the detritus that prevented them from leaving their underground prison. On the failure of Whetmore and the defendants to return to their homes, the Secretary of the Society was notified by their families. It appears the explorers had left indications at the headquarters of the Society concerning the location of the cave they proposed to visit. A rescue party was promptly dispatched to the spot.

The task of rescue proved one of overwhelming difficulty. It was necessary to supplement the forces of the original party by repeated increments of men and machines, which had to be conveyed at great expense to the remote and isolated region in which the cave was located. A huge temporary camp of workmen, engineers, geologists, and other experts was established. The work of removing the obstruction was several times frustrated by fresh landslides. In one of these, ten of the workmen engaged in clearing the entrance were killed. The treasury of the Speluncean Society was soon exhausted in the rescue effort, and the sum of eight hundred thousand frelars raised partly by popular subscription and partly by legislative grant, was expended before the imprisoned men were rescued. Success was finally achieved on the thirty-second day after the men entered the cave.

Since it was known that the explorers had carried with them only scant provisions, and since it was also known that there was no animal or vegetable matter within the cave on which they might subsist, anxiety was early felt that they might meet death by starvation before access to them could be obtained. On the twentieth day of their imprisonment it was learned for the first time that they had taken with them into the cave a portable wireless machine capable of both sending and receiving messages. A similar machine was promptly installed in the rescue camp and oral communication established with the unfortunate men within the mountain. They asked to be informed how long a time would be required to release them. The engineers in charge of the project answered that at least ten days would be required even if no new landslide occurred. The explorers then asked if any physicians were present, and were placed in communication with a committee of medical experts. The imprisoned men described their condition and the rations they had taken with them, and asked for a medical opinion whether they would be likely to live without food for ten days longer. The chairman of the committee of physicians told them that there was little possibility of this. The wireless machine within the cave then remained silent for eight hours. When communication was reestablished, the men asked to speak again with physicians. The chairman of the physicians' committee was placed before the apparatus, and Whetmore, speaking on behalf of himself and the defendants, asked whether they would be able to survive for ten days longer if they consumed the flesh of one of their number. The physicians' chairman reluctantly answered this question in the affirmative. Whetmore asked whether it would be advisable for them to cast lots to determine which of them should be eaten. None of the physicians was willing to answer the question. Whetmore then asked if there were among the party a judge or other official of the government who would answer this question. None of those attached to the rescue camp was willing to assume the role of advisor in this matter. He then asked if any minister or priest would answer this question, and none was found who would do so. Thereafter no further messages were received from within the cave, and it was assumed (erroneously, it later appeared) that the electric batteries of the explorers' wireless machine had become exhausted. When the imprisoned men were finally released, it was learned that on the twenty-third day after their entrance into the cave Whetmore had been killed and eaten by his companions.

From the testimony of the defendants, which was accepted by the jury, it appeared that it was Whetmore who first proposed that they might find the nutriment without which survival was impossible in the flesh of one of their own number. It was also Whetmore who first proposed the use of some method of casting lots, calling the attention of the defendants to a pair of dice he happened to have with him. The defendants were at first reluctant to adopt so desperate a procedure, but after the conversations by wireless related above, they finally agreed on the plan proposed by Whetmore. After much discussion of the mathematical problems involved, agreement was finally reached on a method of determining the issue by the use of the dice.

Before the dice were cast, however, Whetmore declared that he withdrew from the arrangement, as he had decided on reflection to wait for another week before embracing an expedient so frightful and odious. The others charged him with a breach of faith and proceeded to cast the dice. When it came Whetmore's turn, the dice were cast for him by one of the defendants, and he was asked to declare any objections he might have to the fairness of the throw. He stated that he had no such objections. The throw went against him, and he was then put to death and eaten by his companions.

After the rescue of the defendants, and after they had completed a stay in a hospital where they underwent a course of treatment for malnutrition and shock, they were indicted for the murder of Roger Whetmore . . . . In a lengthy special verdict, the jury found the facts as related above, and found further that if on these facts the defendants were guilty of the crime charged against them, then they found the defendants guilty. On the basis of this verdict, the trial judge ruled that the defendants were guilty of murdering Roger Whetmore. The judge sentenced them to be hanged, the law of our Commonwealth permitting him no discretion with respect to the penalty to be imposed.

Author's Comment No. 1 as judge employing some of the concepts upon which this work is based.

If the law-government system of the Commonwealth is the relevant system to deal with the problem of the killing of Whetmore, then it must be determined whether Whetmore's life was taken under circumstances and because of behavior proscribed by the laws of this Commonwealth. However, if it is not the relevant system, then its laws are not relevant to the circumstances and behavior and ought not be employed. The life of an aged Eskimo may be taken by his grandchildren in the northern territories of Canada. Our legal system must take no notice of it or risk violating the sovereignty of the Canadian system. Nor can we take notice of the casting of a deformed baby into piranha infested waters in the jungles of Brazil. Nor can it function in the context of the murder of six million Jews by the Germans. This is not to say that no law-government system has jurisdiction over such behavior or that only one may have; it is only to say that ours does not. The problem is to identify the relevant entirety (group) whose legal system must function upon receiving the input of this case.

The facts are extremely important. Here are five men (all of whom wish to live) without the nutritive means to survive. Together they seek for a means. Individual interest of each to survive becomes the goal of the group. The first precondition of a legal system is present—two or more people associated in joint effort to achieve a common goal. They desire to control or use whatever they have or acquire in order to achieve their goal. What do they have? Apparently only each other. They are informed that outside help cannot be relied upon in achieving their goals. More days will pass in the effort to rescue them from the outside than in which they can survive. For them to preserve individual life and conserve social and economic resources (themselves) they can rely on no others. Whetmore himself devises a plan for survival. It involves controlling and using what each has—the lives of the others—by conserving as much of the social and economic resources available as possible. Four of them shall eat one. They know that such behavior will prolong their lives until they are saved because they have been so informed by experts. In an effort to involve the authority system of the Commonwealth, they requested aid and advice in the decision process to adopt or reject the plan and its mechanics, the casting of dice in choosing the one whose life was to be taken for the sake of the others. Men of science, law, government, and religion refused to participate. Thereby the

Commonwealth's legal system and important parts of its moral and scientific culture were deliberately withdrawn from these men. They were now more alone than ever. No longer was the barrier only physical. It was now also social.

The five men agreed that one of them should die by the casting of dice. A formal irrational decision-making technique, fair and reasonable under the circumstance, because all have an equal chance to live or die, is chosen. All the men are given joint positions of authority in participating in the procedures for decision making. The fairness, morality, and appropriateness of the system is understood and agreed upon by all, each being fully aware of all the circumstances. Indeed, an adequate law–government system is created with heavy reliance on rules of substance and procedure rather than on human whimsy and arbitrariness to implement their goal.

Then a divergency of urges occurs. Whetmore decides to relinquish participation thereby, if he is successful in his challenge, unilaterally and arbitrarily changing the odds on dying or survival for the remaining four. This challenge to the group's legal system has several facets. There is a claim by the four that they be able to control and use what they have (Whetmore) and what they acquire (Whetmore's agreement to participate in his own plan). Further they claim that Whetmore act in good faith by performing his promisory part of the agreement intended to structure relationships between the group members and to fulfill its goals. Whetmore's claim against the group would be that the others not commit aggressions against him as he decides unilaterally his relationships with and obligations toward the others. The conflict and claims are serious. The general security of the group is threatened. If one may act unilaterally, all can act unilaterally. The security of their only social institution (their law–government system founded on contract) is threatened. A suitable morality founded on that contract, arising out of the circumstances and ideally suited to the goal of the group, is violated. Social resources are dissipated and wasted. The general progress of the group in achieving its goals is stultified. And individual life at a level acceptable to the group under the circumstances is threatened. The group's very existence is threatened.

Whetmore challenges the supremacy condition of the law-government system. Unless the group maintains the supremacy of its authority under the contract, it will not be able to act for the benefit of the whole according to the plan with its allocation of authority and procedures, but instead may force a shattering of the group as each is channeled to look out for himself unilaterally. No longer would each be recognized by the others as an official who appropriately may enforce the explicit imperatives of the agreement with applications of legitimate force. Each would be a law unto himself able to survive or die only on the basis of his ability to employ physical force in his desire to stay alive. Each would be quickly reduced to the role of a primitive beast of prey with no socially structured relationships with others of his kind. Or else, all abandoning their desire to live, passive acceptance of the inevitability of death would be followed by certain extinction.

Instead, the other members of the group arose to Whetmore's challenge. He was required to meet his obligations voluntarily assumed strictly accordin to the procedures established. The technique for decision making was extremely appropriate. It was prescribed. And it was compatible with the goals of the group. Social utility criteria were clearly employed in settling this group's one trouble case. The law-government system of this group functioned perfectly in contrast to ineptitude demonstrated by the clearly inappropriate system of this Commonwealth under the circumstances. The Commonwealth's system should not now be allowed to function in this matter. It would have required all of them to die. That is a logical inference from the charges it brought against them.

The four were not members of the Commonwealth. They did not have its problems. They did not share its goals. The officials of our legal system demonstrated as much by their inaction. When challenged to act as officials employing the authority of the Commonwealth, they could not successfully meet the challenge. They would make no decision on behalf of all the citizens of the Commonwealth including the men in the cave. They could not advise the explorers to behave in a manner that would mean certain death for all while tremendous resources in time, money and lives of this Commonwealth were being expended to save them. Nor could they advise on another course.

As for the expenditure of wealth and lives by citizens of this Commonwealth, they are not relevant to the issue (except to note that if the explorers did not act as they did all would have been wasted). Much of our wealth and many lives have been lost in efforts to make the hard lives of the Eskimo and the Brazilian Indians better for humanitarian reasons. Our interest and our efforts on their behalf did not make our law-government system theirs. More wealth and lives were lost by our humanitarians from this Commonwealth in fighting the Axis power to save security and freedom for the peoples of the world, including the Jews; but our efforts did not make our legal system theirs.

The Commonwealth must face up to the fact that its law-government system is limited to the functions relevant to the achievement of its goals.

When another group because of circumstances of geographic, geologic, social, and psychological separation exert joint effort to solve their own problems and achieve their own goals by means most suitable to their own conditions and totally foreign to our problems, goals, techniques, and values, we must have the wisdom not to interfere. No harm can be done to us, our goals, our institutions, or our values. If anything, we benefit from the return of four sound, healthy men to our Commonwealth to retake cherished and productive places in society. No aggressions have been committed against any member of our system. The security of our existence and institutions has not been threatened. No behavior has run counter to our generally accepted moral standards. The restraint called for by such wisdom cannot threaten our existence or our general progress or lead to waste of social resources. No behavior is likely to be channeled to such destructive ends. The members of our Commonwealth know that in the conduct of affairs in the future, each is justified in assuming that no other will commit aggressions against him. Our system in its restraint will not have sanctioned aggression. It is clear.

The only appropriate decision in this case must be based on a recognition of these facts: The five unfortunate men in this cave, by circumstances already alluded to at length, jointly acted to achieve a common goal, the preservation of human life; a divergence of urges among them resulted in a claim of the group that one of its members act in good faith. The claim was recognized and protected by the authority system of the group with an enforcement of the law while relying on all due process requirements. In the complete chain of events, the following functions of law were performed. There was an allocation of authority and procedures which effected an appropriate decision technique by channeling behavior so that in the settlement of one trouble case to arise the goal of the group was achieved. That law-government system worked well. Ours did not work because it was not relevant. Nothing has since happened to make it relevant.

Author's Comment No. 2

A citizen of this Commonwealth, while within the borders of this Commonwealth, was set upon by four men, killed and devoured, all while a fortune in money, countless man hours of effort and the precious lives of ten men were being expended in a Commonwealth-wide joint effort to save his life. A landslide explains these facts. But it does not change them. Nor does a question informally put to citizens while they were in no way acting in their official capacities serve as a vehicle for removing the questioners from the jurisdiction of this Commonwealth. Even if acting officially at the time, momentary ineffectiveness is no excuse for taking the law into one's own hands. The outcome of this case cannot rest on such flimsy and dangerous technicalities.

As a citizen of this Commonwealth, Whetmore was justified in assuming that no one would commit an aggression against his life while he remained within its boundaries and under the protection of its laws; for this is a civilized Commonwealth. In a civilized society one must be able to make such an assumption even if there is no policeman nearby and available. The people of this Commonwealth share certain social interests in common. One is the right to be secure in life according to our community's standards of what is desirable as human and deserving of mankind. Another is to be protected against behavior that runs counter to generally accepted moral standards. Still another is to be secure in its social institutions. Most important is the security to society from those acts that threaten its existence. I can think of no behavior more likely to threaten the very existence of this Commonwealth than for any small group or groups, regardless of how disadvantaged, to set up within this Commonwealth their own legal systems to carry out their own nefarious ends by whatever depraved means they desire. If one group can do it, then another will feel justified also in ignoring the law of this Commonwealth when it suits them. All will be on notice that the authority system of the Commonwealth can be successfully challenged, that in fact it is not supreme, that it represents others only and not them if they choose to separate themselves from the whole. Authority successfully challenged is not authority. Officials are not officials. All and each can become laws unto themselves and then only the naked power of the beast of prey will allow the strongest to survive at the expense of the weak. The structure of society, held together by the thread of law which has developed over the course of history to keep the beast in man at bay so that there can be progress in all the ways in which we use that term will have been destroyed.

Countering the claim of the Commonwealth that willful killing shall not be done within its borders, it is claimed that these men were as divorced from this society, its institutions, goals, and values, as if they were Eskimos or Brazilian Indians. This is a trick in which apples are called oranges or pears. And to claim that the murder of six million Jews was none of the business of the people of this Commonwealth, who function most effectively collectively through their social institutions, is heartless and insensitive. To change the name of a reality does not change the reality. These men were citizens of this Commonwealth, in this Commonwealth. They share its values, goals, and institutions. Its values are theirs. They cannot shed them at will and then expect no reaction from the society threatened by the act. They were still a part of this society in that cave. The time, money, resources, and *lives* spent in saving them is ample evidence of that proposition. To say that those lives are not relevant to the issues of this case is also heartless and insensitive. The technicalities of the claim cannot obscure reality.

Look at the relationships of the men in the cave into which they carried the goals and supporting values, morals, and law of this Commonwealth. An illegal agreement was made and broken. Four men set upon another and kill him, so that they might live—animal conflict at its most base. In no sense can it be regarded as manifesting a divergence of urges among civilized men followed by claims put before an authority for resolution. The pretenders to authority are brutal aggressors only, employing nothing but force and acting only for their own benefit. If they were acting on behalf of the whole group, they could not have killed Whetmore. There is nothing to indicate that Whetmore recognized the four as officials of anything. His acknowledgment that the dice were rolled fairly, allegedly on his behalf, was an academic abstraction. There could be only one reason for the dice being rolled for him. The four hoped that irrational formality would be the vehicle for relieving their consciences of any malicious intent arbitrarily to kill Whetmore. Whetmore desired to participate neither as a cannibal or victim. If he had not lost the throw, he would not have eaten the one killed. They knew this fact. There could be only one significant outcome in the toss of the dice for Whetmore. He could not gain anything. He could lose. He knew this. Therein is no recognition of authority or any law system. Certainly no functions of law could be performed. What behavior channeling could take place? None, certainly, in so short a time. Instead of the implementation of long-term goals, only immediate whim was satisfied by the behavior of the four. The goals of this Commonwealth to save Whetmore's life as well as theirs was obstructed by their behavior. No justice was done. The end did not justify the means.

They are subject to our law–government system and its standards, doctrines, and principles. This being so, the rule proscribing the willful taking of the life of another is relevant, if in fact that is what was done. The law is very specific and clear. It was designed to protect individuals and social interests already mentioned. There is no extenuating circumstance here. These four men did willfully take the life of another. They violated the law. They were not defending themselves from Whetmore's attacks. He was not attacking them. He was not forcing them to kill him in order to save themselves. He only wanted to be left alone and not be forced into behavior that ran counter to his deeply engrained moral standards acquired from his associations with his fellow men in this Commonwealth. His moral sense caused him quickly to repent from the participation in the evil bargain of the group to commit a cannibalistic act. If the others wanted to violate the law by such an unholy contract, it was their risk that they might be held accountable by our legal system upon which Whetmore was relying for his protection.

This is an extreme case, a hard case; but if such a hard case is allowed to change our law, we may be creating a precedent for further weakening changes in the future. Future emotions may find a scintilla of reason in this case to excuse further irrational, immoral, and antisocial acts, which can only imperfectly be anticipated. For example, who knows how far the current rash of student disorders will go or what comfort they will find in the dangerous doctrine that if they do not perceive the social legal system as relevant they may create their own? If these men are not guilty of murder, then the law of murder says that it is unlawful willfully to take the life of another unless a group however small views its interests as different than the interests of the society and views its legal system as inadequate to promote their interests. Whereupon they may by contract establish their own law however repugnant to the law on murder and immunize themselves from the retribution of our legal system, so long as they explicitly follow the terms of the contract.

The Mafia would approve of such a law. If such a drastic change is to be made in our law, it is for the legislature to consider coolly and dispassionatel in its chambers, untrammeled by the emotional appeal of any particular case and strictly upon the basis of a careful weighing of social policies. I cannot be permitted that luxurious choice. I am required to do my duty and apply the law no matter how distasteful it may be to me personally under the circumstances.

The outcome of this case is not in doubt. One may not willfully take the life of another in this Commonwealth else he is guilty of murder. By their own admissions, in addition to great amounts of gruesome physical evidence and even greater amounts of circumstantial evidence, they did willfully take Whetmore's life. Therefore they are guilty of murder.

In arriving at such a conclusion, I recognize that I have employed formal rational techniques for finding and applying law. This is not a case where a substantive rational approach is appropriate. The law is well settled. Social values underlying the law are now as they have been. This is not a case where substance of the circumstances demands of reason that it innovate to achieve a just result, as was done in the case of the exception of self-defense. This is not time or occasion to experiment with the flexibility of law. In circumstances of self-defense, it is highly questionable that the one defending himself is acting willfully. It is far more probable that his act is a socio-psychologically determined act, partly also the result of a fundamental instinct for self-preservation far from an act of free will. In the cave, four men acted with cool, deliberate determination according to a well-developed plan.

No tedious process is necessary to demonstrate that this Commonwealth has a legal system. The preconditions have long been in evidence—group effort toward common goals, occasional divergencies of urges and resultant claims laid before an authority system with the ability to enforce its imperatives for the benefit of all through the carefully prescribed procedures long familiar to us all. No challenge to supremacy of the system has ever been successful, and this one is not going to be. Using appropriate and time-honored decision techniques founded on faithful applications of law, our goals are well served by this very successful legal system. There can be only one legal system in the Commonwealth. That entity is the Commonwealth itself. It follows that there is only one legitimate bolder of authority. Again it is the Commonwealth. That authority is now being exercised.

Furthermore it must be recognized that this decision is the only possible socially acceptable one if emotion can be avoided in the decision process. Preventive channeling of conduct to avoid future similar trouble cases is one result. Securing of individual expectations that aggressions will not be committed against them is another. Protection of society from behavior that runs counter to accepted moral standards necessary to the continued existence of our society and its institutions is the ultimate long-term goal implemented. Justice is done.

U.S. v. HOLMES[3]

Holmes was a seaman on the William Brown, which set sail from Liverpool for Philadelphia in 1841. The ship struck an iceberg some 250 miles from Newfoundland and soon began to sink. Two boats were lowered. The captain, various members of the crew and a passenger got into one of them and, after six days on the open sea, were picked up and brought to land. The other boat was called the "long-boat"; it was leaky and might easily be swamped. Into it Holmes jumped along with the first mate, seven other seamen, and thirty-two passengers—about twice as many as the boat could hold under the most favorable conditions of wind and weather. Just as the long-boat was about to pull away from the wreck, Holmes, hearing the agonized cries of a mother for her little daughter who had been left behind in the panic, dashed back at the risk of instant death, found the girl and carried her under his arm into the long-boat. The sailors rowed and the passengers bailed, but the overweighted long-boat, drifting between blocks of floating ice, sank lower and lower as a steady rain fell on the sea. The wind began to freshen, the sea grew heavy, and waves splashed over the bow. Then, after the first mate had twice given the order, Holmes and the rest of the crew began to throw the male passengers overboard. Two married men and a little boy were spared, but the fourteen remaining male passengers were cast over, and two women—devoted sisters of one of the victims—voluntarily leaped to join their brother to his death. The long-boat stayed afloat. The next morning Holmes spied a sail in the distance, exerted himself heroically to attract notice of the passing vessel, and eventually brought about the rescue of everyone left in the boat.

When the survivors arrived in Philadelphia, the mate and most of the seamen, hearing talk of prosecution, disappeared. Holmes was put on trial for manslaughter.

In his charge to the jury as to the law, the judge stated that passengers must be saved in preference to all seamen except those who are indispensable to operating the boat. If no seaman can possibly be dispensed with, then the victims must be chosen from among the passengers by casting lots, provided—as in this case—there is time enough to do so.

The jury found Holmes guilty but recommended mercy. He was sentenced to six months' imprisonment at hard labor, in addition to the nine months he had already spent in jail awaiting his trial.

NOTES

1. Regina v. Dudley & Stephens, Queens Bench Division, L.R.14QBD273 (1884).

2. Fuller, Lon L. "The Case of the Speluncean Explorers" 62 *Harvard Law Review*, (1949), 616-619.

3. U.S. v. Holmes, 262 Fed. Cas. 360 (c.c. ED.P. 1843).

BIBLIOGRAPHY

The works upon which this book is based are Harold D. Lasswell, *Power and Personality* (1948); Neil J. Smelser, *Sociology of Economic Life* (1963); Roscoe Pound, *The Spirit of the Common Law* (1921); Pound, *Introduction to the Philosophy of Law* (1922); Pound, *Jurisprudence* (1960); Karl Llewellyn, "The Normative, the Legal, and the Law Jobs: The Problem of Juristic Method" (1940); Llewellyn and Hoebel, *The Cheyenne Way* (1941); Llewellyn, *The Common Law Tradition* (1960); Max Weber, *Law in Economy and Society,* ed. Max Rheinstein (1954); Robert A. Dahl and Charles E. Lindblom, *Politics, Economics and Welfare* (1953).

Other works cited in this book are Edmund N. Cahn, *The Sense of Injustice* (1949); Jean Piaget, *The Moral Judgment of the Child* (1969); Gordon Tullock, *The Logic of Law* (1971); Kenneth M. Stamp, *The Causes of the Civil War,* (1959); Daryl J. Bem, *Beliefs, Attitudes and Human Affairs* (1970); Lasswell and Kaplan, *Power & Society* (1950); Peter Bachrach and Morton S. Barhtz, *Power and Poverty* (1970); Wesley M. Hohfeld, *Fundamental Legal Conceptions,* ed. W. W. Cook (1946); John C. H. Wu, *Cases and Materials on Jurisprudence* (1958); *Blacks Law Dictionary* (1951); Karl Llewellyn, "What Price Contract?" (1931); Sir Frederick Pollack, *Section Seventeen of the Statute of Frauds* (1885); Oliver W. Holmes, Jr., *The Common Law* (1881); Kai T. Erikson, *The Wayward Puritans: A Study in the Sociology of Deviance* (1966).

Jurisprudence as a general topic is treated in the following: John Austin, *Lectures on Jurisprudence* (5th ed., 1885); Jeremy Bentham, *Limits of Jurisprudence Defined,* ed. Everett (1945); Edgar Bodenheimer, *Jurisprudence* (1960); Huntington Cairns, *Theory of Legal Science* (1941); Sir Frederick Pollock, *Essays in Jurisprudence and Ethics* (1882); Pollock,

A First Book of Jurisprudence (4th ed., 1918); Sir John Salmond, *Jurisprudence* (10th ed., 1948); George W. Paton, *A Text-Book of Jurisprudence* (2d ed., 1951); Bodenheimer, *Jurisprudence, the Philosophy and Method of the Law* (1962); Thomas A. Cowan, ed., *American Jurisprudence Reader* (1956); Carl J. Friedrich, ed., *The Philosophy of Law in Historical Perspecti* (1963); H.L.A. Hart, *The Concept of Law* (1961); Roscoe Pound, *An Introduction to the Philosophy of Law* (1959); Paul Vinogradoff, *Historical Jurisprudence* (1920); Hedley H. Marshal, *Natural Justice* (1959); C. Mullins, *In Quest of Justice* (1931); Rudolf Stammler, *Theory of Justice* (1925); Harry T. Allan, "Questing for a Jurisprudence for the Millions: Some Parameters," *American Business Law Journal* 10 (1972).

Works dealing with instrumental and primary goals and law include A. Denning, *Freedom Under the Law* (1949); Marc A. Franklin, *The Dynamics of American Law* (1968), a textbook with case material drawn from freedom of expression cases; John S. Mill, *On Liberty* (1859); Perry, ed., *Sources of Our Liberties* (1959).

Works specializing on the subject of power and employment of power or alternatives include Robert L. Hale, "Force and the State," *Columbia Law Review*, 35 (1935), 1949; Thomas V. Smith, *The Ethics of Compromise* (1956); William J. Chamblis, *Law, Order and Power* (1971).

General works on the nature of legal systems include Benjamin N. Cardozo, *The Nature of the Judicial Process* (1921); Cardozo, *The Growth of the Law* (1924); H.L.A. Hart, *The Concept of Law* (1961); Roscoe Pound, "The Limits of Effective Legal Action,"*Ethics,* 27 (1917) 150; Malcolm Sharp, "The Limits of the Law" *Ethics* 61 (1951), 270; A.S. Diamond, *Primitive Law* (1935); Jerome Frank, *Law and the Modern Mind* (1949); Jay A. Sigler, *An Introduction to the Legal System* (1968); Giorgio del Vecchio, *The Formal Basis of Law,* trans. Lisle (1914); John Honnold, ed., *The Life of the Law* (1964); Lewis Mayers, *The Machinery of Justice: An Introduction to Legal Structure and Process* (1963); Adamson Hoebel, *The Law of Primitive Man* (1954); M.P. Golding, *The Nature of Law* (1966) Carl A. Auerbach, ed., *The Legal Process* (1961).

The subject "functions of law" figures prominently in the following works: H. Richard Hartzler and Harry T. Allen, *Introduction to Law; A Functional Approach* (1969); Robert S. Summers and C. G. Howard *Law, Its Nature, Functions and Limitations,* 2d ed. (1972); Harold Berman, *The Nature and Functions of Law* (1958); H. Lauterpacht, *The Function of Law in the International Community* (1933); Julius Stone, *The Province and Functions of Law* (1946).

Specialized works dealing with recognized officials called judges include Irving Rutter, "The Trial Judge and the Judicial Process," *Journal of Legal Education,* 15 (1963), 245; James Willard Hurst, "Who Is the Great Appella

Judge?" *Indiana Law Journal,* 24 (1949), 394; Evan Haynes, *The Selection and Tenure of Judges* (1944); Bureau of Municipal Research, *The Magistrates' Court of Philadelphia* (1960); Institute of Legal Research, University of Pennsylvania, *Toward Judicial Reform in Pennsylvania* (1962); Morse Erskine, *The Selection of Judges in England: A Standard for Comparison, Journal of the American Bar Association* 39 (1953).

Specialized works on the decision process include Lon L. Fuller, "Adjudication and the Rule of Law," *1960 Proceedings of the American Society of International Law* (1960); Clarence Morris, *How Lawyers Think* (1938); Paul Vinogradoff, *Commonsense in Law* (1913); Morris R. Cohen, *Reason and Law: Studies in Justice Philosophy* (1950); Fuller, *Legal Fictions* (1967); Julius Stone, *Legal System and Lawyers' Reasonings* (1964); William Zelermyer, *The Process of Legal Reasoning* (1963); Edward Levi, *The Process of Legal Reasoning* (1957); Karl Llewellyn, *The Bramble Bush* (1951); Judith Shklar, *Legalism* (1964); Fuller, *The Law in Quest of Itself* (1966).

Works that focus on fact determination include Clarence Morris, "Law and the Facts," *Columbia Law Review,* 22 (1922), 1.

Works that integrate some of the areas covered in this book include Graham J. Hughes, ed., *Law, Reason and Justice* (1969); Arnold M. Rose, "Sociological Factors in the Effectiveness of Projected Legal Remedies," *Journal of Legal Education,* 11 (1959), 470; Leland Hazard, "Social Justice Through Civil Justice," *Journal of the Chicago Law Review,* 56 (1969), 699; Huntington Cairns, *Law and Social Sciences* (1935); M.R. Cohen, *Law and the Social Order* (1933); Eugene Ehrlich, *Fundamental Principles of the Sociology of Law* (1936); Roscoe Pound, *Law and Morals* (1924); Pound, *Social Control Through Law* (1942); W.A. Robson, *Civilization and the Growth of Law* (1935); M. Schoch, ed., *The Jurisprudence of Interests* (1948); Sidney P. Simpson and Julius Stone, *Law and Society* (1948); N. S. Timesheff, *An Introduction to the Sociology of Law* (1939); Roscoe Pound, *The Formative Era of American Law* (1938); Carl A. Auerbach, "Law and Social Change in the United States," *UCLA Law Review,* 6 (1959); 516; Loren C. Eiseley, ed., *Social Control in a Free Society* (1960); William M. Evan, *Law and Sociology* (1962); H. Kelsen, "Law as a Specific Social Technique," *Journal of the Chicago Law Review,* 9 (1941), 75; Pound, *Social Control Through Law* (1942); Pound, *Law and Morals* (1923); L.M. Friedman and S. Macaulay, *Law and the Behavioral Sciences* (1969); Jerome Frank, *Law and the Modern Mind,* 2d ed. (1949); Otto Kirchheimer, *Political Justice: The Use of Legal Procedure for Political Ends* (1961); F. A. Whitlock, *Society, the Offender and the Psychiatrist* (1966); Ray D. Hensen, ed., *Landmarks of Law,* (1960); June L. Tapp, and Lawrence Kohlberg, "Developing Senses of Law & Legal Justice," *Journal of Social Issues* 27 No. 2 (1971).

INDEX